The Cultural Subversion
of the Biblical Faith

The Cultural Subversion of the Biblical Faith

LIFE IN THE 20TH CENTURY
UNDER THE SIGN OF THE CROSS

by
JAMES D. SMART

THE WESTMINSTER PRESS
Philadelphia

BOOK DESIGN BY DOROTHY ALDEN SMITH

First edition

Published by The Westminster Press®
Philadelphia, Pennsylvania

PRINTED IN THE UNITED STATES OF AMERICA

9 8 7 6 5 4 3 2 1

Library of Congress Cataloging in Publication Data

Smart, James D
   The cultural subversion of the Biblical faith.
   128p. ; 21 cm.
      1. United States—Religion—1945—   2. Christian-
ity—United States. 3. United States—Civilization—
1945—   I. Title.
BL2530.U6S63   209'.73   77–22063
ISBN 0–664–24148–4

Contents

Foreword

The concern of this book is with the contradiction that exists in all our Western nations between the Biblical faith to which Christians are or ought to be committed and the policies they support in their national life which in this twentieth century have brought the world to the edge of an abyss. Something is wrong. Something is desperately wrong. And we may not have very much time to discover what it is. We seem to have been afflicted all through this century with a peculiar blindness. We had no difficulty in the '30s in recognizing the disastrous blindness of our fellow Christians in Germany who gave Hitler his opportunity—our evangelical fellow Christians, among them some distinguished theologians, even some who signed the Barmen Declaration. But where our own nations and their policies are concerned we can be equally blind and yet remain totally unconscious of it. This book is an attempt to explore the nature and the sources of this blindness, which has led to the cultural subversion of the Biblical faith. It will indicate the perils to which we are exposed and suggest the better future that might be possible for our world were Christians to be guided in their public policies by a genuinely Biblical faith.

The problem is international and inescapable for Christians in every nation. Most of us were born into both a Christian community and a national community, a Christian tradition and a national tradition, a Christian culture and a

national culture. The two elements mingled in us from our
earliest years and merged imperceptibly, so that we have
usually been unaware of where the line of distinction between the two occurs in us or which is more weighted than
the other. We have tended to take for granted that, because
we are Christians, our culture is a Christian culture and our
citizenship a Christian citizenship. This merging was for a
long time almost automatic everywhere in Western civilization, both in Europe and in North America. Western civilization was assumed to be Christian civilization and our countries all of them to be Christian countries. But the events of
the twentieth century have set all such optimistic evaluations
radically in question. National cultures that long prided
themselves on their Christian character have shown a disturbing ability suddenly to take on a directly anti-Christian
character. And in more than one country, Christians in the
hour of testing have found the national element in their
citizenship much stronger than the Christian element. Loyalty to a national tradition has taken precedence over the
Christian tradition, which at its heart calls for unconditional
loyalty to Jesus Christ in the whole of life. Therefore, it is a
time for all of us to examine ourselves and find where in us
the line runs between the Christ of the cross and devotion to
our nation.

The problem being international, why then does this book
approach it as though it were more acute in America than
anywhere else? Surely it would be more pertinent, more
scholarly, and more valuable to investigate it in a wider
range of Western nations. The author being a Canadian, why
does he not make the Canadian phenomenon the basis of his
inquiry? To that I must answer that I can speak to the problem only as I have experienced it personally in my ministry
in Canada and the United States. Such is the nature of this
blindness that it was only when I had come awake to it in the
United States that I began to be aware of its presence in a
somewhat different form in Canada. My ministry has been
divided almost half and half between the two countries, and

I find myself deeply involved in the life of both. Citizenship for me has long been a North American citizenship. Therefore, since this problem surfaced for me during my years in the United States, and since it is perhaps more visible there as well as more dangerous, the power of the United States being what it is, my attention has been focused mainly on the American phenomenon. To discuss the problem in more general terms would have been like preaching a sermon on sin in general when some very specific sin had shown itself in the local situation. When Cross and Nation were embattled in Germany in the '30s of this century, a scholarly investigation of the conflict of loyalties in the citizenship of Christians in general would have been rather innocuous. German theologians had to speak to the problem as they knew it in themselves and in their own nation. Other Christians listening in could spell out for themselves the implications for their own situation.

The present development of "civil religion" in the United States will be the starting point for our investigation, but only the starting point. Quite recently Martin Marty delivered a public lecture on that subject in Canada. On a television interview he made the remark that some Canadian theologians had assured him there was no similar development or problem in Canada. Certainly we have no "civil religion" movement, but we have the problem of which that is just one visible expression. Nationalism takes a very different form in Canada than in the United States. Since Canada is divided between two cultures and the whole land mass of the nation falls into five sharply divided areas with strong sectional loyalties and interests, the lack of a unifying national spirit has long been a serious matter. But close below the surface, the contradiction between Cross and Nation exists in several different forms. In Quebec, French-Canadian nationalism has now become a religion with its prophet and its holy scriptures; it threatens to take precedence over all other loyalties, either Christian or Canadian, and to tear Canada apart. In English-speaking Canada a British nationalism, which both provoked the French-Canadian nationalism and impeded the development of a distinctive Canadian national consciousness, has always assumed an essential identity of Christian and British traditions. Then, with the ever-greater merging of the Canadian and American economies and cultures, many in our population share with Americans the inclination to identify North American democracy with Christianity.

There is no room for self-righteousness or pointing of the finger here in discussing what can only be called a massive failure of Christian citizenship in the twentieth century. We have all been guilty of a confusion of loyalties that has blinded us to the realities of our world and has let us stumble into one disaster after another. The problem is particularly acute in the United States because of its present eminence as a world power and the dependence of so many countries, including Canada, on its decisions and attitudes. Also, because of a certain refreshing American openness and frankness, the problem here attains a high degree of visibility once one begins to be aware of it.

J.D.S.

Introduction

The chapters of this book were originally four lectures delivered at the Northwestern and Alaska Conference of the American Lutheran Church in April, 1976. The chosen theme for the conference, I was informed, was "Civil Religion." I was not told whether the choice of theme indicated a critical or a supportive stance. In fact, not having encountered the recent discussion of the subject, I was not at all clear what I was being asked to discuss. As a Canadian, six years removed from active participation in the American scene, I had missed this debate. But I soon discovered that under another name the issue had been long familiar to me. During my years in the United States as an editor of church school educational materials, what now was being called civil religion had been known in my staff as our most stubborn enemy, the widely pervasive popular American religion, diverse in its forms but always essentially nationalistic, which made it so difficult to secure consideration for a sharply defined, positive Christian faith.

One highly sophisticated expression of this religion was John Dewey's *A Common Faith* (1934), a humanist religion in which American democracy took over the place occupied in Christianity by the Kingdom of God and the attempt was made to preserve the ethical values of the Kingdom without any of the distinctive Christian doctrines. The public schools were naturally the shrines of this religion, and since many

public school teachers taught also in church schools, their
strongest inclination was to teach the same religion there,
merging it as much as possible with their Christianity. Confronted with materials that spelled out distinctly the difference between a humanist and a Christian faith, they were
often bewildered, and in their bewilderment sometimes
found their pastor as confused as themselves by the suggestion of a conflict between the two.

More often this religion appeared in a cruder form as an
identification of Christianity with the American way of life.
The confrontation with Communism after 1945 brought this
version strongly to expression. I remember specially a conference of two thousand church school teachers, directors of
Christian education and ministers in 1947 in Des Moines,
Iowa, under the auspices of the International Sunday School
Association, where this identification seemed to be the primary conviction of most persons present. The whole Western world at that time, in the aftermath of the 1939–1945
war, was in the grip of a hysterical dread of Communism.
What was needed from the church was a word that could
conquer fear and send into public life leaders who would face
the problems of postwar reconstruction and healing with a
clear Christian vision. But of the four key speakers at that
conference three contributed mainly to an intensification of
the fear. Their common theme was that the American way
of life, Western civilization, and the Christian faith, all in one
lump and with no clear lines of distinction between them,
were being drastically imperiled by Communism. They
called for a crusade by the churches and church schools of
North America to save us from this doom. It seemed to be
taken for granted that the American way of life in its religious, political, and economic character was the primary expression and the primary custodian of Christianity for the
whole world.

To me that confusion of a national culture with the Christian faith was a far more serious threat than Communism to
the future of both the American people and the Christian

church. Atheistic Communism was a peril at a distance and easily recognized, but the intrusion of a nationalistic religion into the churches and church schools was a peril close at hand, immediate and menacing, which would corrupt the church at its very heart if it were not recognized and withstood. Therefore it was urgent that Christians should have their eyes opened to the contradictions between this muddled version of the Christian faith and a faith that takes seriously its continuity with its origins as they are discoverable in the Scriptures.

In 1955, Will Herberg laid the problem open for all to see in his book *Protestant—Catholic—Jew*. He showed how widely churches and synagogues had been invaded by a religion that had been stripped of its distinctive Protestant, Catholic, and Jewish features. He alleged that beneath a formal adherence to their doctrines the real religion of the majority of the members of all three institutions had become an amalgam of values and ideals from various sources, welded together with patriotism in the national consciousness to form its religious foundation and made generally acceptable to many Christians and Jews by the invoking of the name of God.

Robert Bellah, who initiated the more recent discussion of this problem in 1967 under the banner of "Civil Religion," approached the matter from a stance almost directly opposite to that of Herberg. For Bellah the need of the hour in America was for a religion sufficiently free of all distinctive institutional markings that it would be found acceptable and inspiring by all Americans. A religious undergirding seemed to him to be essential to the stability of every society. For many generations Christianity had served as the cement to hold the American nation together and give it direction. But now in a pluralistic society it was no longer adequate and there were ominous signs of disintegration. A common faith was needed, a faith that could be shared by all Americans, Christians and non-Christians alike. Then came Bellah's joyful announcement that a common faith of this kind had long

been present and needed only recognition. He traced the
presence in American history of a religion that was not primarily of the churches but of the nation, whose priests and
prophets had been Presidents such as Jefferson and Lincoln
(and in a lesser degree many others), whose places of pilgrim-
age have been the graves of Presidents and the blood-stained
scenes of national conflict, and for which the schools have
served ably as centers of propagation. The time was now
come to give it a respectable name, "civil religion," and to
recognize it as a religion in its own right, no longer to be
confused or merged with Christianity or Judaism. In fairness
to Robert Bellah, one must point out that in a later publication, *The Broken Covenant: American Civil Religion in Time
of Trial* (1975), he attempts to distinguish between a tenable
and an untenable form of civil religion and rehearses its
history from the very beginning to show how crudely nationalistic it can be. He also acknowledges that it has been an
empty shell except when a revival of evangelical religion has
given it a nobler content. But his critique of civil religion in
its past does not in any way discourage his project for the
building out of a more respectable form of it in the present
and future.

These proposals set a wholly new discussion in process
which since 1967 has produced a considerable literature in
articles and books and has been forwarded by a number of
conferences. In 1972 the Southeastern Baptist Theological
Seminary in cooperation with the American Jewish Commit-
tee sponsored a gathering at Wake Forest University which
explored a variety of approaches to the subject. In Novem-
ber, 1975, the Religious Education Association made it the
theme of its annual conference and devoted two issues of its
journal to the discussion. A surprising number of Christian
theologians, alarmed at what to them was a shaking of the
very foundations beneath the national life, seemed to find
Bellah's proposals attractive. Civil religion appealed to them
as the answer to an urgent need: a religion that could be
taught in the schools, and a glue that would hold the nation

together. But in all the literature on the subject, any sharp exploration of the theological issues that underlie the whole situation has been strangely absent.

There is a danger that what meets us here may seem to be just another of those theological discussions of recent years that for a moment have commanded a wide interest, have produced a flood of literature, and then have faded from the scene. The debate on Bultmann's demythologizing proposals left with us a whole shelf of essays and books. So also did the discussion of Bishop Robinson's "Honest to God," a rather muddled amalgam of the ideas of Tillich, Bultmann, and Bonhoeffer that nevertheless for many people brought out into the open in everyday language some of the Biblical and theological issues that were engaging the interest of theologians. On the heels of Robinson came the "death of God" debate with its rather inane theatrical flourishes (a television funeral service for God with choristers in tears) and its use of language that confused rather than clarified the actual situation of most people in their thinking concerning God. Then in quick succession came the "Secular City" debate, begun by Harvey Cox but very soon deserted even by him as he found other questions more important, the "theology of hope" inspired by Moltmann's book, and the "theology of liberation" which in some degree has been an outgrowth of the theology of hope. Placed in this succession the civil religion debate may seem much more ephemeral than any of its predecessors. All of them have been international in their scope and interest, while civil religion by its very nature has seemed to be an American phenomenon and an American problem. Each of the earlier discussions has been focused on a question of such depth and importance that, while it may have commanded wide attention only for a few moments, it must remain a long-continuing concern of the church for generations. But surely civil religion is an option so transparently at odds with any intelligent commitment to the Christian faith that it hardly merits any very serious inquiry. Leave it alone and it will soon be forgotten.

This, however, is to misjudge both the breadth and the depth of the problem. In the Foreword we have seen that it is a deeply rooted international problem. Two books, Robert T. Handy's *A Christian America* (1971) and Martin Marty's *Righteous Empire* (1970), help us to see that it has been with us for centuries. Both books trace the history of the American church and nation back across the centuries to their origin in Britain and show how, in spite of an official doctrine of the separation of church and state developed later, both church and state have been dominated continuously by a religious conception of the nation and its destiny, so that religious devotion and national loyalty have long tended to merge. The roots of this merger lie in sixteenth-century Britain, where British Christians so identified themselves with the Israel of God in the Scriptures that they transferred from church to nation the promises of God to Israel. Even more vivid was the identification with Israel of those who left the old land to found a new nation in America. Their journey across the Atlantic paralleled for them the exodus from Egypt. Their new home was the Promised Land. Their future was the future promised by God to a faithful Israel.

Thus the dream that inspired the life of American churches for three centuries was that here at last was to be founded a really Christian nation, Christian not just in name but in the character of its life and in the unfolding of its destiny. For a considerable portion of the history this was conceived as a Protestant Christian nation, and Catholics were barely tolerated as an alien factor, while Jews were ignored. With the increase in Catholic population and a decrease in religious antagonisms, the adjective "Protestant" fell away, but until recently it was still customary to speak of "a Christian nation," and it is not long since we experienced a crusade "to make America Christian." By the middle of the twentieth century, however, the intolerance of that language was becoming generally apparent. To the millions of Jews, to the adherents of other religions, and to those in the population who professed no religion, it was less than courteous, it was untrue, and it was damaging to national unity for Christians to speak as though the nation belonged by right to them alone. It was in part this recognition of the pluralistic character of American religion, coupled with a fear that the nation, without a common religion to bind its citizens together, would begin to disintegrate, that gave birth to the present project to launch an independent American civil religion, so defined that it would command the loyalty of all Americans and preserve unsullied and unshaken the traditions on which the nation was founded.

This development, however, takes on another and even more serious complexion when we draw into consideration the present relationship between North and South America. Again two books have broadened the scope of inquiry: Gustavo Gutiérrez' *A Theology of Liberation* (1973) and José Míguez-Bonino's *Doing Theology in a Revolutionary Situation* (1975). These books take us into the present South American situation and let us look through the eyes of a Catholic and a Protestant theologian at the revolutionary forces developing in the churches, and beyond the churches, there. But, more important, they shock us awake to the fact that for the submerged masses to the south of us our North American society, economically and culturally, has the character of an all-powerful oppressor. These theologians see their whole world—their economy, their culture, their churches—imprisoned and denied a future by their dependency relationship with our North American–European power complex, in short, with our capitalist-oriented Western civilization. From their first settlement the South American people were dominated and exploited by a Spanish elite that held its privileged position by grace of Spain. In the nineteenth century, in adulation of Western democracies such as Britain and the United States, South American nations in general broke with the old order and dreamed of a similar process of development in the southern hemisphere to that which had produced prosperity and freedom in the north. But now masses there are awaking to the fact that they have merely exchanged their dependency upon Spain for a dependency upon the lords of Western capitalism, who find it expedient to cooperate with the same thin upper crust of elite in South America who for so long have kept the masses in subjection. Even our most generous loans and gifts to stimulate their economy enrich mainly those who retain their traditional positions of advantage. With galloping inflation, the lower levels of population sink ever deeper into poverty, misery, and cruel subjection to ruthless dictatorships, dictatorships that find no difficulty in securing the cooperation of our governments.

Seen through the eyes of Latin-American theologians of liberation, who are committed by their understanding of the gospel to the freeing of their world from such subjection to us, civil religion in the United States must look like a cunning religious construction superbly designed to lend a divine validation to the whole order that holds them and their people enslaved. Seen from inside our society it may appeal to us as an excellent device to propagate and safeguard in our population the bare minimum of religious and ethical principles necessary for the survival of a civilized democratic society, but from the outside, from the hovels of South America, from almost anywhere in the Third World, it may have the appearance of a theological instrument of tyranny. That consideration gives our subject an additional international significance and makes it extremely urgent that Christians in America should look very closely at this phenomenon of civil religion, not brushing it off as the latest theological fad but recognizing its crucial importance and its deep-rootedness in our past. The integrity of the faith that we profess is at stake in this consideration.

1

A Nation with the Soul of a Church?

It may help to get our problem more clearly out into the open if we begin by listening to several people, theologians and others, for whom the civil religion advocated by Robert Bellah has in it not peril but promise. The historian Sidney Mead has long regarded America as, in G. K. Chesterton's phrase, "a nation with the soul of a church" and has perhaps set a higher valuation upon the religion of the nation than upon the religion of the churches. Mead quite rightly insists that a nation is a spiritual society, that it "is what it is in virtue of a common mental substance resident in the minds of all its members—common memories of the past, common ideas in the present, common hopes for the future, and, above all, a common and general will issuing from the common substance of memories, ideas, and hopes" (in Russell E. Richey and Donald G. Jones, eds., *American Civil Religion,* 1974, p. 48; quotation from Ernest Barker, *Church, State and Education,* 1957, p. 136). Mead finds most congenial Tillich's dictum that religion is the substance of culture while culture is the form of religion, and for him culture comprises all the highest elements in the nation's life. Therefore, American religion can no more be equated with the American way of life than Christianity can be equated with the way of life of present-day Christians. Both by their nature transcend any existing order.

The religion of the Republic, like Christianity, is essentially prophetic, with ideals of justice and equality that bring present injustices and inequalities under judgment. It is *natural* religion in contrast to the *revealed* religion of the churches, and this natural religion, says Mead, holds fast to "what is essential in every religion," essential in the sense of what is necessary to the health and preservation of the society concerned. Benjamin Franklin, with his belief in God as Creator and Providence, and in goodness, immortality, and a moral order, had a firm hold on the essentials of natural religion. General Eisenhower's statement about the importance of religion to the nation, and his seeming unconcern about what religion it should be, expressed the mood of a Franklin or a Jefferson, a traditional American mood. The essentials of religion being thus defined, it is at least hinted that the doctrines of revealed religion are not in any way essential to the health and well-being of the larger society beyond the churches. Then, when Mead tells with evident approval that for Lyman Beecher the nation had the function of a church, in fact, is the primary agent of God's meaningful action in history, and that the national creed has "theonomous cosmopolitanism" at its core, it begins to look suspiciously as though civil religion based on natural revelation has captured a preeminence that lets any church religion based on a Biblical revelation fade into the background. But what would this civil religion be without any of the elements that have flowed into it from the Biblical tradition?

A quite different advocacy of civil religion is found in Richard John Neuhaus' *Time Toward Home: The American Experiment as Revelation* (1975). He appreciates Bellah's achievement in focusing interest upon the subject of civic piety and insisting upon its importance for the nation's future. But he deplores Bellah's abandonment of the tradition union with "the Judeo-Christian gospel of the Kingdom" (p. 188). He wants equal emphasis upon both Biblical and civil religion. "The most promising gamble, I believe, is the interplay between explicit biblical religion and the American tradition of public piety. . . . They exist in a symbiotic relationship, each supporting and, to some extent, checking the other" (p. 19). "As a false religion, Americanism must be repudiated; as the piety of a people 'under God,' Americanism must be purified and revitalized" (p. 190). Civil religion is no more than "a halfway house of belief and morality" (p. 190), but necessary since not all will accept Biblical religion. It lies at the very basis of the nation's life, and neglect of it has contributed substantially in recent years to a weakening of the moral and spiritual fiber of the population. "What is called civil religion requires the sustained, serious and explicit attention of the best minds both within and without the churches, both within and without the academic community professionally concerned with religion" (pp. 189f.). Neuhaus can say with Bellah that "there is in American society a vague but real cluster of symbols, values, hopes and intimations of the transcendent which overarch our common life" (p. 201), but for him this is not a religion with its own independent life. He has no sympathy with Mead's definition of it as "the transcendent universal religion of the nation," nor with J. Paul Williams' proposal that governmental agencies should teach the democratic idea as religion. But he is willing to attribute to democracy an absolute value that is "not unlike 'the Will of God' " and to say that "democracy should be inculcated with religious seriousness *for the Kingdom's sake*" (p. 204). And he finds a revelation of God in the American experience.

What Neuhaus wishes to combat is the mood of despair, disillusionment, and disgust with all forms of patriotism which has captured wide sections of the population since the early '60s. This mood, however, has been generated not just by the idiocy of the Vietnam war, the rebellion of the counterculture, and the shock of the Watergate exposures, as he seems to assume, but at a much deeper level by an accumulation of crises in Western civilization. The technological advances that were to launch a Golden Age have suddenly taken on a character that threatens the human values of our world. A society dependent on oil for its survival wakens one morning to find the whole order of its life in peril and itself at the mercy of the oil-producing countries. Keynesian deficit financing was to have made depressions no longer possible, but now most lands are in a bind with a combination of depression and inflation at the same time and are desperate to discover any way out. Lawlessness increases year by year. Dictatorships multiply steadily. The number of the nations in which freedom of thought, speech, and action is restricted and tortures are used to secure the obedience of the citizen has mounted steadily where half a century ago the triumph of democracy was confidently expected. A church that in the '20s was out to conquer the world has since 1945 found itself to be a minority movement even in the Western world where it was once so confident of victory and is having to rethink its whole approach to the task of evangelizing the world. World population soars, and soars most quickly in those regions of the world that are least equipped to provide even a bare sustenance for this larger society, much less an opportunity for a decent life for the members of a future generation. And all the time there hangs over our world the hydrogen bomb, threatening to wipe out most of our problems by a swift annihilation.

It is little wonder that many ask themselves whether what we are living through is the first stage in the breakup of Western civilization. Arnold J. Toynbee has taught us that civilizations are born, mature, grow old, and die, and that how soon they die is determined by how they meet the challenges to their existence. We can see the dimensions of the challenges that now confront us. How we meet them is yet to be determined, but certainly a mood of despair spells death. Neuhaus is right that despair and disillusionment must be overcome and that something more than civil religion is needed if that is to be achieved. What that something more is he does not say too clearly. At one point, as we have seen, he calls it "the Judeo-Christian gospel of the Kingdom," a phrase not likely to be acceptable to either Jews or Christians. He wants to generate a patriotism, a love of country,

a common faith, a civic piety, that will not degenerate into
nationalistic idolatry, nor find itself in contradiction to a
healthy Christian or Jewish faith. This, after all, is certainly
the problem. But when he is done, there still remains a
strong suspicion that he has not faced adequately the problem of how the lion that resides in civic piety is to be prevented from swallowing up the lambs of Christian and Jewish
faith.

An equally strong plea for civic piety has been made by
Robert W. Lynn in an article in the *Religious Education*
journal for January-February, 1973. A Presbyterian theologian, he harbors no fears concerning the possible future development of a patriotic civil religion such as Bellah envis-
ages, independent of both Christianity and Judaism. Bellah,
he says, has "celebrated the virtues of American civil religion
at its best." He has no word of criticism for Bellah. Neo-
orthodoxy is said to have been responsible for a serious neglect of civic piety." This is a strange judgment when one
thinks of Karl Barth and Reinhold Niebuhr as representatives
of neo-orthodoxy: Barth whose theology generated in
Europe a quality of citizenship that withstood the temptations of the Nazi era, and Niebuhr who in America for a
generation forced his contemporaries to rethink their approaches to the problems of the community.

Like Neuhaus, however, Lynn is troubled by the seeming
disintegration of the religious principles that underlie the
daily life of the American community. He quotes the church
historian Sydney Ahlstrom, who traces the beginnings of despair and confusion to the experiences of the depression in
the '30s and finds them mounting steadily during the intervening years to become "a crisis of loyalty" in the '60s. Neither Lynn nor Ahlstrom seems to take adequate account of
the international phenomena that have contributed to the
mood of despair, to distrust of governments everywhere, to
revolt against the technological establishment, and to a questioning of the whole economic order of our Western world.
The sickness of our society is no slight disorder in American

civic piety, to be remedied merely by the encouragement of those virtues which make up the substance of Bellah's civil religion.

One can agree with Lynn as he quotes Paul Lehmann: "Without piety there can be no justice; and without justice there can be no commonwealth." The religious and moral principles to which men and women are committed are the foundation of the nation's life. The critical review of those principles and the inculcation of them at every level in the community is a concern of every loyal and intelligent citizen. Most of Lynn's essay is devoted to a description of McGuffey's Eclectic Readers as a model of what can be done at the elementary levels of education. (A Canadian parallel to McGuffey's Readers would be the series of Golden Rule Readers which were my own introduction to culture and an encouragement to high resolves parallel to and complementing what I experienced in church.) But surely the ideals and visions of the future encouraged by McGuffey do not constitute a religion, a civil religion, that must have an existence independent of one's Christian or Jewish religion. Lynn's approval of Bellah's radical proposal is perplexing, for at no point in his essay does Lynn even discuss the relationship of this independent civil religion to the Christian or the Jewish religion, nor does he say how one is to operate with two religions, one civil and one more than civil.

Lynn's accusation that neo-orthodoxy contributed heavily to the dissolution of civic piety in America requires an answer because it has on the surface of it a certain plausibility and at the same time points to a deeper issue in American theology which has never been adequately exposed and clarified. Many of the theologians who are roughly lumped together as neo-orthodox have, by their recovery of their roots in a Biblical faith, been made either uneasy or openly critical of the traditional blending of church and nation that has long been characteristic of civic piety. What few, however, have recognized is that basic to this blending is a much more profoundly theological mixing of Biblical revelation with natural revelation. This comes out quite clearly in Neuhaus' book. He insists on a messianic conception of America's destiny, in line with three hundred years of civic piety, and uses as the subtitle of his book *The American Experiment as Revelation.* He then denounces Jacques Ellul and William Stringfellow for their branding of this way of thinking as idolatry.

Both Mead and Bellah recognize frankly that what they are claiming as the ultimate authority for their civil religion is a natural revelation of God *in the American experience* quite independent of the Scriptures. This begins to suggest to us why North American theologians, even some who would be called neo-orthodox, have tended consistently to defend at least some vestige of a natural revelation as basic to Christian thinking and Christian existence, some knowledge of God that man—American man, Western man, religious man—has in independence of the revelation of God to which the Scriptures testify. But always this natural revelation, however vestigial, turns out eventually to be the fortress in which man defends himself and his human achievement against the devastating critique that issues from the Scriptures. Forty-four years ago in Germany it was a revelation of God *in the German experience* that provided the legitimation for theologians such as Friedrich Gogarten and Gerhard Kittel to lend their support to the Nazi rebirth of the nation. And it was the spelling out of the antithesis between natural revelation and the Biblical revelation by such theologians as Karl Barth that laid the foundation for the Confessional Church and its resistance to Hitler.

Barth's unpopularity in America, even among many Reformed theologians, has perhaps been due to their unease at his rejection of natural revelation. Emil Brunner, who left the door open a small crack to natural revelation (which permitted him to make the future of the Christian church dependent upon the survival of Western civilization), has usually been preferred to Barth as representative of Reformed theology. So deep-rooted is this commitment to natural theology, far below the level of conscious thought, that for many American theologians it is as though Barth were pulling the rug out from under their feet. But the issue will eventually have to be faced if the church of Jesus Christ in America is to have its freedom to be truly itself.

In Richey and Jones's *American Civil Religion,* Will Herberg has a chapter on "What It Is and Whence It Comes." In 1955 he wrote as a Jewish theologian, with strong Christian sympathies, who saw in the popular American national religion an alien force that was invading churches and synagogues, blotting out everything that was distinctive in Jewish and Christian faith. Twenty years later he writes more coolly as a student of religious phenomena and describes civil religion as the American state religion, parallel to the state religion in ancient Greece and Rome. It is a system of allegiances, norms, and values that give the nation the unity necessary for survival. For most Americans it is simply the American way of life. It is not the common denominator of religions in general but a distinctive American development with its own character—the national life apotheosized, the national heroes divinized, and the national history experienced as salvation history—a blend of Supreme Being, ideals, morals, individualism, brotherhood, optimism, pragmatism, faith in education, high valuation of sanitation, disparagement of culture in any aesthetic sense, commitment to democracy and free enterprise. Puritanism and revivalism are secularized to produce a strenuous idealistic moralistic religion but with no sense of sin or judgment; active, pragmatic, promotional, with "deeds, not creeds" as its motto. To some this is *the* comprehensive religion of America in which each of the individual religions should have its place, as in the Pantheon in Rome.

Herberg finds among most Americans today no sense of conflict between civil religion and separate faiths. Confessional resistance, he says, has been steadily eroding and disappearing. There are small holdout groups of theologians but "by and large, the great mass of Americans are not aware of any tension or friction or conflict between America's civil religion and their professed faiths, whatever they may be." In his final evaluation Herberg classifies it as a genuine state religion, similar to the Athenian or the Roman, "a noble religion celebrating some very noble civic virtues" and "the best way of life yet devised for a mass society." But not for one moment, he says, is it to be seen as authentic Christianity or Judaism, and to set it above or in place of those religions is nothing less than idolatry.

CHRISTENDOM AND CHRISTIAN NATIONS

The concept of Western civilization as Christendom and of the nations participating in it as Christian nations has lain at the root of many of our illusions about ourselves. What must puzzle us today is that it should have persisted so far into the twentieth century and should still exert such influence in the thinking of many Christians. The idea dies very hard that our culture is essentially Christian and that our nation is basically a Christian nation. We inherited Christendom from the Middle Ages and it was such a comforting and reassuring concept that we have clung to it as though we would be naked without it. In the medieval structure of the Western world there was no firm line of separation between church and state. Civil and religious interests were closely interwoven. Religious heresy was regarded as a peril to both church and nation. All citizens were marked by baptism as Christians before they could dispute that identification. Only Jews could escape, and at times not even they. It was ostensibly a Christian world and the name for it was Christendom.

As nations developed their independent existence, it was taken for granted that they were Christian nations, even when they went to war against each other. With the Protestant revolution, while churches and nations broke free from Roman authority, they did not break free from this medieval unity of church and nation, under which the citizen could no more determine his own religious loyalty than his commitment to the state. Diversity of religion was everywhere seen as an endangering of the unity and stability of the body politic. Thus, in seventeenth-century Britain, Anglicans, Presbyterians, and Congregationalists fought bloody battles to determine what form of Christianity would be established in the realm, and, one form being established, there was no longer freedom for any other. But no one would have questioned then or for centuries afterward that Britain was a Christian nation. Britain, France, Germany, Italy, Holland, Spain, Russia—all were Christian nations. Not until the '20s of the twentieth century did that judgment begin to be seriously questioned. The whole thinking of Christians was determined by the division of the world into two halves, Christendom and the non-Christian lands beyond. There were Christian nations and there were non-Christian nations.

The American people through the centuries experienced a specially intensive form of this orientation, and, in the mid-twentieth century, with 65 percent of the population registered in the membership of church and synagogue, they persisted in thinking of themselves as a Christian nation long after the idea had faded almost everywhere else. The first settlers in New England must have had doubts about how Christian England was, since they had been denied freedom there for the exercise of their religious convictions, but they were determined that the nation they would establish in America would have full right to the name.

At first they had no more toleration for variant forms of Christianity than their persecutors had in the old land. Only gradually did toleration win its way and citizenship find a freedom in separation from church membership. But, as Robert T. Handy has shown so graphically in *A Christian America*, there was not, either then or for centuries, any slackening in the determination that America should be Christian and, as a Christian nation, should fulfill the destiny that in Scripture is promised to the Israel of God. Even a Jefferson with his rationalist religion thought of his nation as a modern Israel and cherished for it a messianic future. Here on this continent would be built the New Jerusalem, a demo-cratic New Jerusalem, and from it would go out healing influ-ences that would eventually transform the life of the whole world. As Handy has shown, under the influence of this vision Christian history in America has consisted of one crusade after another, each geared in its own way to establish one more feature of a Christian America. In 1950, with such a high percentage of the population on church rolls, there seemed reason for a fair measure of confidence in what had been achieved.

But by 1950 the very concept of Christendom and Chris-tian nations had become incredible for anyone who was awake to what was happening in the world. Two world wars within thirty-one years, each leaving in its wake a sea of misery and devastation, plus a collapse of the worldwide economy that wrecked the lives of millions, and all of this in countries that had been called Christian, shattered the old assumption. More influential than anything else was the fact that in one of our "Christian" nations, the center tradition-ally of Christian theology and of many of the finest achieve-ments of Christian civilization, the most brutal and inhuman order emerged, sent six million Jews to their deaths in gas chambers, and threatened to take over the mastery of Europe. This put an end to the facile labeling of any nation "Christian." A Western civilization that in less than half a century could produce such a succession of horrors was cer-tainly not a Christian civilization in contrast to other cultures but had to be recognized as what it had always been, an order of life composed of contradictory forces, some Christian and some the very opposite of Christian. No realistic assessment of any of our national societies could validate the placing of the label "Christian" on them. In America the Vietnam war, so inexcusable, and the struggle of blacks for their freedom, so bitterly resisted, shocked wide sections of the population awake to the non-Christian heart concealed beneath the sur-face profession of devotion to justice and benevolence. A majority of the population in the membership of the church does not give a nation the right to call itself Christian.

We have, therefore, to interpret against this background the disillusionment and mood of despair over America that has troubled Bellah, Ahlstrom, Lynn, and Mead and made them turn to civil religion as a remedy for what seemed to be a disastrous gap in the national foundations. From a Christian standpoint the disillusionment must surely be pronounced a healthy phenomenon, a coming awake of America to the reality of its own life, a dispersal of illusions, something similar to a Christian repentance. Nothing has caused more confusion in America's relations with other nations in recent years than the self-righteousness that sets a Christian America over against a non-Christian world, a just and righteous America over against an unjust and unrighteous Communism. Before God we have to be what we are, a sinful nation like all others, a groping, stumbling, blind, well-meaning but selfish nation, intent upon its own advancement, idealistic yet at the same time ruthless in promoting its own interests. In God's name let us not meddle with the present mood of disillusionment, for if it means that America is losing its self-righteousness and self-justification, it can be the necessary preliminary to a new and better future. The justification that is the product of a humble faith is a far healthier phenomenon than any form of self-justification, not only in individuals but also in communities.

What one says here of America is equally true of other lands, such as Canada and Great Britain, and not of them alone. The illusion of "Christendom" was productive of a colossal self-righteousness all across our Western world. Civilization and Christianity were interchangeable words. We were the civilized and Christian nations in contrast to the uncivilized and unchristian areas of the world. It was unquestioned that missions must both evangelize and civilize, and civilize meant superimposing our order of life upon the evangelized society. The generosity that prompted the mission tended to conceal the self-righteousness about our order of life that was implicit within it. In theological seminaries in the '20s of this century it was taken for granted that, if one had a first-degree commitment to Jesus Christ, one naturally volunteered for service in the foreign field; second degree, one went to Western Canada; third degree, one sought a church in Central Canada where the communities were already quite civilized and Christianized. It was this kind of thinking that made it possible in Britain to interpret the building of the British Empire as the product of a kind of evangelical benevolence, a sharing of the blessings of our order of life with less fortunate peoples. And the same kind of thinking lends justification to the twentieth-century spread of the American empire.

Also, the acknowledgment that our nations are not Christian nations does not entail a blindness to the Christian influences and virtues at work in our society, nor does it lessen our love of country, our appreciation of its achievements, or our determination to do everything in our power to make our communities more Christian, more humane, than they are. In fact, nothing would do more to release and promote a genuine, healthy patriotism than the vanishing of that false patriotism which feeds on self-justification. Christians are released to be good cooperative members of a pluralistic community when they remember that they share a sinfulness and a responsibility for the sins of their society with all the non-Christians. In the same way, a nation is released to be a good cooperative member of a world society of nations when within its citizenship there is willingness to drop all pretensions of moral superiority and to be just one among the many nations in which wisdom and folly, virtue and vice, humanity and inhumanity are constantly struggling for the mastery.

It becomes ever clearer as we proceed that our real subject is not American civil religion but something much more universal and of concern to every Christian. That we focus on America is merely because, thanks to Robert Bellah, it is there that the problem has been brought out so clearly into the open. Our task is to explore the nature of Christian citizenship and the implications of the Christian faith for the total life of any nation. Since the foundations of everything Christian are to be found in the unfolding of the life of a people of God as it is exposed to us in the Scriptures, we shall have to weigh constantly what they say to us. And as the whole subject opens up in its full breadth and depth, we shall perhaps begin to see what it is that has been neglected and so has encouraged such a lush growth of civil religion.

Has American Protestantism tended to concentrate its attention upon what it calls the soul or the spiritual side of life, so that it has left a great gaping religious vacuum in the bodily, external, public life of the nation? Has there been in many people's minds a radicalization of the separation of church and state, far beyond anything intended by the Constitution, a separation so absolute that Christian thinking stops short at the border of the state and leaves that whole territory to be occupied by the spokesmen for various forms of civil religion? Insofar as we have concerned ourselves with Christian citizenship, have we let our perspective be bounded by the national borders, so that our concern for justice stops short at that point and does not touch our economic and political dealings with the rest of the world? Is there a split personality in many Christians, an earnest Christian faith operating in one sphere of their existence while civil religion is operative with an equal earnestness in a second sphere, the two merging where they have common elements, so that the Christian is not even conscious of the split in his being? Questions such as these make clear the necessity that we should establish much more definitely the implications of a Biblical faith for our present-day citizenship.

THE DIMENSIONS OF THE PROBLEM

It may have value, before we go directly to the Scriptures for light on our problem, for me to describe how the larger dimensions of the subject opened up as I began to look into

it. Three books and the recollection of two incidents became
for me windows into the situation.

The first stimulus came from a chance reading, from which
I had not expected much, of the *Memoirs* of the Hungarian
cardinal archbishop, Jozsef Mindszenty. I knew him only
from the newspaper accounts of his enforced sojourn for
many years in the American legation in Budapest, a fugitive
from the Communist government. I thought of him, none too
respectfully, as mainly an apostle of the postwar anticommu-
nist crusade rather than as the defender of any essential
Christian principles—the defender, rather, of traditional
Roman Catholic special advantages in Hungary. That may
have been because of the McCarthyite character of the people who rallied round him on his visits to the United States
after he had gained his freedom. But in his memoirs I found
him before all else a passionately devoted churchman with
a high conception of his responsibility as archbishop and as
primate of Hungary, not just for the defense of the church
but for the welfare of the Hungarian people. His conduct as
archbishop was unacceptable first to the Fascist government
and then to the Communist. He was imprisoned by the Fascists, who cooperated with Hitler, as well as by the Communists, who were under the thumb of Stalin. His later refusal
of Rome's request that he demit his office brought to expression his conviction that he was appointed not just by Rome
but by God as shepherd over the Hungarian people. What
interests us, however, is that both Fascists and Communists
in Hungary drew a solid line between church and state, between religious and secular realms, and warned Mindszenty
not to interfere by word or action in the area they considered
to be under the sole authority of the state. The education of
youth was a function from which the church was excluded,
so that all church schools were taken over by the government. And Mindszenty refused to recognize the line.

Undoubtedly at some points Mindszenty was defending
traditional privileges of the Roman Catholic Church that
belonged to an old, outdated order. But he was denied any

real freedom to exercise his care over the life of his people. The line drawn between state and church imprisoned him in the church but it did not protect him from interventions by the government in the life of the church. His basic care was simply that his people should remain Christian in their citizenship. When they were starving he made their plight known to the rest of the world and received help chiefly from America. When Russian military forces prevented the Hungarian people from having the government of their own free choice, he protested with all his might. He refused to be silenced and as a consequence became first a prisoner of the Communist government and then a fugitive in the United States legation. On his release to live in Vienna he spent the remainder of his years traveling about the world as a shepherd of Hungarian Catholics who were scattered in exile.

Mindszenty's significance for us lies in his refusal as a Christian to recognize any absolute line of separation between church and state. He was operating on the basis of a central Christian doctrine that is as central for us as it was for him, the sovereignty of God over the whole of man's life. To surrender his right to exercise a care over the whole life of his people was to surrender his faith and to betray his office. Where we as Protestants must be critical of Mindszenty is in his absolutizing of his authority over the life of Hungarian citizens through his simple identification of his sovereignty as primate with the sovereignty of God. This is a centuries-old Catholic tradition from which Protestants have suffered discrimination and deprivation in lands where the government has been in close alliance with the Catholic Church. In reaction to such forms of oppressive religious absolutism, and thinking to secure an area of freedom for every form of religious conviction, Protestants have tended to go to the opposite extreme and to draw a line between church and state, between the religious and the civil realms, a line that, when it is made absolute, denies not just the church but God himself his sovereignty over the life of the citizen and leaves in the civil sphere a vacuum that is then a temptation to various forms of political absolutism.

The experience in Hungary, Russia, and other eastern countries should be a warning to us against any loose talk of "an absolute line of separation between church and state." Wherever Christians shut themselves in behind a line of that kind and leave a religious vacuum on the other side of the line, there is likely always to be a temptation toward dictatorship, and, as in Russia, the church ceases to exert any appreciable influence upon the public life. Of course, there is always another possibility, that an absolutist church and an absolutist state may find it to their mutual advantage for a time to make common cause and to divide between them the profits of their partnership at the expense of a population that has lost its freedom. As Protestants we can have no sympathy with the absolutizing of any human authority, political or ecclesiastical. The sovereignty of God, far from authorizing, actually relativizes all such human authorities, and it dissolves all lines of separation that men draw between areas of life, civil and spiritual. Christians must be on their guard when any such line is drawn and suspicious that citizenship is about to be defined by some form of civil religion or civil philosophy of life that is distinctly *not* the Christian faith.

A second book that influenced my thinking was a collection of papers presented by German and American scholars at a conference in Indiana on "The German Church Struggle and the Holocaust." They were edited by Franklin Littell and H. G. Locke and published in 1974. The conviction of those who sponsored this conference was that the world has not yet profited adequately or taken sufficiently to heart the German experience of the '30s and '40s of this century. "A study of American high school textbooks in 1961 showed that their treatment of Nazism was brief, bland, superficial and misleading. The Holocaust, if mentioned at all, was discussed in a few lines which usually transformed millions shot or gassed into thousands mistreated or killed, and organized mass-murder became merely an excess of traditional Jew-

hatred." Wilhelm Niemöller, a historian of the church struggle in Germany, repudiated the facile assumption, "Hitler
could not happen here." He asserted, "I was and am of the
opinion that Hitler waits and lurks everywhere in some form
or shape."

The most disturbing presentation, however, was by Eber-
hard Bethge, the friend and biographer of Dietrich Bonhoeffer. We have tended in general to glorify the Confessional Church of the '30s as a heroic defense of the gospel
against the demonic pretensions of a totalitarian regime, and
certainly it was a bold protest for the sovereignty of Christ
over his church and against every attempt of the political
power to limit or negate that sovereignty. But Bethge
pointed out that the protest limited itself too much to the
defense of the church. There were no protests in March,
1933, against legislation establishing a dictatorial order, excluding Jews from the civil service, and banning Jews from
the theological faculties in the universities. Bethge quotes a
letter from Karl Barth lamenting that he did not, like Bonhoeffer, see the Jewish question as central in 1933 and 1934.
The Confessional Church had its greatest strength in 1934,
when it was contending with the heresy of the German
Christians who, with the help of some distinguished theologians, were producing a form of the Christian religion that
would lend support to the Nazi new order. But in 1935, when
the government itself began to intervene in the church and
what was necessary was *resistance to the government,* there
was a serious decline of membership in the movement.
There was an unwillingness to disobey state laws. Then in
1938, when with the Crystal Night there began, with state
permission, a persecution of Jews, there was a dead silence
on the part of the church even in the region of the Confessional Church. Bethge makes the claim that "the resistance
movement had no program for political freedom."

What we begin to see here is the operation of a traditional
doctrine of an absolute separation between church and state,
the two-kingdom theory. There were individuals such as

Bonhoeffer who resisted politically, but the church movement as a whole disowned them. How radically that is true is evident at an incidental point. It was the custom in the confessional churches to have intercession lists on which were placed the names of those who were suffering because of their membership in the movement, but names such as that of Bonhoeffer were refused a place on the lists because their imprisonment and suffering were for political action rather than for defense of the church. Here was a principle the exact opposite of the Catholic one that we saw at work in the case of Mindszenty, a refusal to take any action that could be construed as an intervention of the church in the political realm. A church that claimed in its confession to be exalting the Lordship of Jesus Christ over the life of his people was drawing an absolute line between itself and the state in such a way that it imprisoned itself politically and socially and paralyzed itself as a servant of God's justice and compassion in the life of the community. Six million Jews could be rounded up and carried off to the gas chambers, and even this Confessional Church, with its zeal for obedience to Jesus Christ as the Christian's only Lord and Master, thought it dared not speak a word of public criticism. Could anything demonstrate more powerfully to us the peril of drawing a line between church and state that leaves a vacuum in the realm of the state, a religious vacuum that invites the erection of a civil authority with its own religious basis, which may have little or no concern for either justice or compassion?

That, however, was a situation in the past and distant from us. It is easy to make such judgments at a distance. Therefore let us place alongside it a recent incident in our own American religious history that establishes a disturbing parallel between what happened in Germany and what can happen here. In the Christmas season of 1972 President Nixon ordered a bombing of Hanoi which to many American Christians, and not only Christians, seemed a pointless and heartless escalation of the Vietnam war. A Presbyterian minister in Chicago wrote a letter to the Reverend Billy Graham in which he asked him, as the Christian minister closest to the President, enjoying his respect and having free entry to him, to confront him with the character of his action and to make a prophetic protest against it. He received no answer. Dr. Campbell of Riverside Church in New York then took up the cause and preached a sermon he called "An Open Letter to Billy Graham," which did elicit an answer, and both sermon and answer were published in the journal *A.D.* It is the answer that interests us here. In it Dr. Graham asserted that as a minister of Jesus Christ he was called to be a New Testament evangelist with a commission to save souls, not an Old Testament prophet intervening in political matters. His ministry to the President, he also said, was a private pastoral one, not open to public observation and not subject to the scrutiny or criticism of anyone.

This incident is significant not just as it concerns one man but as it reflects an attitude that is widespread and influential in the churches of America. Billy Graham is not to be made the whipping boy for his response, but rather we should be grateful that his honest answer brings out into the open a deeply entrenched feature of our American Protestantism that, if we tell the truth, has in some degree influenced all of us in our ministries. What is commoner in the preaching heard in our churches than that the attention is confined to what is considered the purely spiritual side of life, the inner life, the qualities of Christian character, the availability of spiritual resources for living? These must indeed have our attention, but only their rightful share of it. When they monopolize our concern and leave no room for the more dangerous kind of preaching in which we spell out the implications of the Christian faith for the controversial issues that confront our members as citizens of the community, they then by what they exclude produce a defective, corrupt, and unbiblical gospel. Such preaching also produces a church membership that expects all political and economic questions to be absent from sermons. And, from expecting, it is only a short distance to demanding that it be so.

Graham's distinction between a New Testament evangelist commissioned to save souls and an Old Testament prophet who intervenes in political matters not only disrupts the unity of the Christian canon of Scripture, letting the most essential and central elements in the Old Testament fall away and lose their authority, but also conceals the prophetic character of Jesus' own ministry. Graham is not the only one who fails to recognize the truth that, whatever more Jesus is, both he and John the Baptist are prophets of Israel. Far too many books on the prophets of Israel include only Old Testament prophets and thereby conceal the fact that, after a gap of five hundred years, the prophetic line came to an explosive rebirth and consummation in John the Baptist and Jesus of Nazareth. Jesus speaks of himself as a prophet and more than once classifies himself as belonging to the same category as John. They are children of the same wisdom (Luke 7:35), endowed with the same kind of authority (Luke 20:1-8).

The marks of the prophet are all over Jesus' ministry: Jesus' continuity with the Servant of the Word in Isa., chs. 49; 50; 53; 61, his call to the Israel of his time to recover its destiny as a people bound so deeply and completely to their God that God's very nature would shine forth in them, his bold initiative in breaking with a static religious order and recovering in himself and his followers the prophetic understanding and reality of faith, his expectation that, like the prophets of earlier centuries, he and his disciples would be persecuted, and finally his confrontation of the nation at its center in Jerusalem which resulted in his crucifixion. If Jesus had confined himself to a ministry of saving souls, he could have gone on with it for years without much likelihood of serious interference. It was his prophetic mission to the nation that got him into trouble. Separate Jesus from the whole prophetic tradition, wipe out the prophetic element in his ministry, and he is no longer the Jesus to whom the New Testament witnesses. As a prophet, Jesus also would have protested against any separation of the soul from the body, the inner life from the outer life. His gospel, like that of all who preceded him, is concerned with the whole person and the whole of each person's life in community. Therefore, to be called by Jesus to share in his ministry must be not just a commission to save souls but embarkation on a mission in which the prophetic and the evangelical are inseparable.

It will hardly be disputed by anyone that in wide sections of American Protestantism that pride themselves upon their evangelicalism the prophetic and the evangelical are torn apart in this way. Strangely this rupture is usually performed by Christians who profess to be equally zealous for the authority of the *whole* of the Scriptures! What they do not realize is that they have not only emasculated the ministry of Jesus so that it is incomprehensible why he would be crucified, but they have created a religious vacuum in the secular public area of life that encourages the development there of a secular civil religion, which may then either exist by itself or be combined by church members in an unholy union with their purely spiritual "soul religion."

An experience of my own several years ago illustrates the consequences of this development. At a time when controversy about both the Vietnam war and the racial issue was intense, I was asked to participate in a ministers' conference in a Southern state. The ministers were Presbyterian, Southern Baptist, and Lutheran, and they came from four or five adjacent states. They had points of agreement and disagreement, but on one point they were unanimous—that any word of criticism by them from the pulpit, either of segregation or of the government policy in the war, would make them no longer acceptable as pastors of their congregations. Some claimed that they would be discharged within twenty-four hours. Could anything be more shocking in the church of a Jesus Christ who was crucified for saying what his fellow citizens did not want to hear? I myself had spent the larger part of my ministry in a church in which the freedom of the pulpit was one of its most cherished traditions; not that this freedom has never been challenged, but the awareness is still alive in the membership that, in a church standing in the succession of the prophets and the apostles, with Jesus at their center, one may expect from time to time to have even one's most cherished political and economic as well as religious convictions set in question. But here were ministers whose congregations knew no such principle as the liberty of prophesying!

How could such a paralyzing disaster befall Christian churches? This false tradition must have been taught them, and taught them from the pulpit, with all the authority of being the gospel and the clear teaching of the Scriptures! It must have been taught them for generations to be so deeply rooted! What were they taught? They were taught that both the minister of the gospel and the church as a whole have no other task than the saving of souls, that the church should be kept purely spiritual by avoiding all involvement in public issues. But the issue they should now be facing is whether on the basis of Scripture a church that silences the prophetic voice of its pulpit has any right to call itself Christian. Such a church invites the same disastrous history that overtook the German church in the days of Hitler. It isolates the public life of its land from the scope of the gospel and thereby encourages the development of a national civil religion that could, in a crisis, become the basis of a tyrannical order.

The third book I offer as background for our study of civil religion takes us far back into the days when the Christian religion was invading the Roman Empire, but it provides some very interesting parallels with our present situation. In 1940, Charles N. Cochrane, an authority on Greek and Roman history and literature and at the same time a highly competent theologian, published his *Christianity and Classical Culture,* in which he takes us into the ancient world of Greece and Rome and brings it alive for us in all the details of its daily life and its institutions. At the same time, he exposes the theological roots of its existence. We no longer see it as a museum piece but as a world of human beings parallel with our own, a civilization quite as impressive as ours and strikingly similar to it in many ways. And as he penetrates beneath the surface to the underlying theology on which it was based, to its understanding of God and man and to the consequences of that understanding in shaping men's actions and the structures of the society, he seems to be describing not just the ancient world but also in a considerable measure our modern Western world.

The civil religion on which the Roman Empire was constructed was not too different from the civil religion of our own day. The emperors, of course, were not only its priests but in time became its divinities, the incarnation of what that Roman world took to be divinity. The parallel to this in what Bellah calls civil religion, with Presidents as its priests, may throw some light on the mystic aura that seems immediately to surround an elected President, sometimes with serious consequences for his whole entourage. The pretensions of a society encourage similar pretensions in the head of the society. The Romans too were confident that the civilization they had evolved was superior to all others and that they were conferring an inestimable benefit on less developed peoples in sharing it with them, though the legions were usually necessary to enforce the sharing—and the benefits came at a price that was quite profitable to Rome.

Cochrane, having let us find ourselves at home in the Greek and Roman world, then portrays the invasion of that world by the Christian gospel and church. At point after point the new order of life that issued from the gospel set in question the old classical order. The contradictions were not on the surface alone but were the consequence of a radically different understanding of God, man, and the world. Cochrane located the revolutionary, world-changing dynamic of the Christian movement in its theology, and specifically in its unique understanding of God that comes to formal expression in the doctrine of the Trinity. The Christian located his God not only in the creator and sustainer of all that is but also in the Word, which sets sharply in question the whole established order of life, generating hope of a radically new order, and in the Spirit, which is God as creator and critic taking over the place of rule in the believers' existences and in the life of the believing community in order to achieve his purpose.

In the descriptions of civil religion by Bellah and by Will Herberg, while belief in a God is considered essential, there is no room for any such God as requires a doctrine of the Trinity for the description of his reality. A God is needed as the transcendent support of the whole structure. But from Cochrane we learn something of crucial importance: that a state or civil religion that makes room for a God and has the highest official of the state as its high priest gives to its God the character of being the primary reinforcement of the established order. The deity is being used to validate the values and ideals of the culture, to give a divine aura to the civilization and to set the mark of divine approval upon the way of life that is congenial to the citizens. But the Christian God does not let himself be so used. It is essential to his nature that he sets a question mark against *every* established order. His thoughts are not our thoughts, nor his ways our ways. Our world belongs to him, but his intention for it, evident in the first chapters of Genesis as well as in Jesus' gospel of the Kingdom, brings all its fairest constructions under judgment, a judgment that has in it at the same time the promise of a much more humanly livable world. That promised world is not just a haunting dream, never to be realized, but is the new age that broke in upon our world in the person of Jesus Christ. It was foreshadowed and anticipated in "the community of the remnant" in Israel, anticipated in real faith. The joy of that faith comes to vibrant expression in Second Isaiah and in the Psalms. But in Jesus Christ the glory of God's new age, God's new humanity, became visible in our world. That new humanity was not a private thing. By its very nature it burst forth to embody itself in a community. It was shared by Jesus with his disciples and in them moved out swiftly, in spite of all hindrances, to change the world. Cochrane reminds us that that invasion was not so much an evangelistic campaign as a theological revolution.

The Christian movement from its beginning was not content to become merely the private religion of individuals, bringing a new life to their souls, but leaving the world outside to have its structures determined by whoever at the moment might have the political power. It was intrinsic to the gospel, and intrinsic to the prophetic faith of Israel with which the gospel was so closely linked, that it could be content with nothing less than a new *world*.

The parallel, then, between the state religion of Rome and the civil religion of America, the similarity in their idealism and in the mixture of confidence and anxiety in their outlook on the world, suggests to us the opportunity of the church. Bellah performs a valuable service in making clear once and for all that the civil religion of America is not to be confused with Christianity. It is another religion, the religion of a semipagan civilization, the religious bulwark of a proud political and economic empire—that waits to be redeemed. It has hope of being redeemed only by a church that rediscovers in its strange doctrine of "God in three persons" the power of a revolutionary faith with which to invade the contemporary world. The resistance to such an invasion is theological, both in the world and in the church itself, and only a church that is responsibly coherent in its theology has any hope of making an impact upon a world so confused that only too often neither Christian nor non-Christian is able to recognize the difference between the current civil religion and the Christian faith.

2

The Use and Misuse of Scripture
in Defining Christian Citizenship

We have been concerned thus far to understand the phenomenon "civil religion," to see it for what it is and to explain why it has had such a lush growth in the American scene. But this has given a negative and largely critical character to the discussion, the primary intention of which is a constructive exposition of a Christian citizenship that takes seriously its Biblical foundations. Civil religion is a temptation for Christians that must be decisively rejected. This cannot be seen with full clarity until we have explored the length and breadth of the pattern that emerges from the Scriptures.

The critical survey was necessary. The problems with which we are dealing needed to be put in a larger perspective. Merely to recognize that civil religion is actually "state" religion calls up parallels with state religions in the past that are illuminating and suggestive. The tendency of American pietism to confine the attention of Christian preaching to the soul or inner life suddenly loses its peaceful, harmless aspect when set against the tragic history of the Evangelical Church in Germany in the days of Nazism. Christians need to be shocked awake by Bellah's discernment that the religion operative in the public sphere and invoked constantly by public spokesmen is *not* either the Christian or the Jewish religion but a distinctive American creation with its own history, ritual, and creed. Protestants need to be alerted to the fact that many of them share with the Communists the practice of drawing a sharp line and building on it a wall between religion and politics, between the sacred and the secular, between the church and the state. The Communists do it in order to prevent Christian interference with the building of a Communist society, the Protestants in order to keep religion undefiled, purely spiritual, free of governmental interference, uncontaminated by political concerns. Civil religion itself we recognized to be an amorphous, chameleonlike entity, constantly shifting in character, impossible to control and with a built-in tendency at the slightest provocation to harden into a passionate nationalism. Most dangerous of all for the church, as Will Herberg warned in 1955, civil religion intrudes itself into Protestant and Catholic churches and into synagogues, only too often determining or coloring the message of the pulpit and shaping the mind of the pew, displacing any genuine and vital Christian or Jewish convictions. Perhaps the most serious intrusion has been into the church schools.

We have now to bring this whole area of concern under the light of the Christian gospel. What have the Scriptures to say to us as a Christian church and as Christian citizens concerning our responsibility in relation to the problems we must constantly face and the decisions we have to make in the public realm? But first, what is the proper way to use the Scriptures, that it may be the gospel of God that we hear from them and not just a reflex of what we most want to hear? We have already in one instance had a warning that Christians may hear in their reading of the Scriptures only what supports their established religious stance.

THE BEGINNINGS IN AMERICA

We must begin our investigation with the pioneers who three and a half centuries ago in New England laid the first foundations of this nation. For them at least there was no sharp line that could be drawn between church and state, between a religious and a secular realm. For them the entire life of the community was under the sovereignty of God and had to find its direction from the word of God in Scripture. But they were not open to the possibility that different groups of Christians might hear the message of the Scriptures differently. Because they were fugitives from oppression we tend to expect them to have been apostles of freedom and tolerance. Since they had experienced in the old land the rule in the political and social realm of a form of Christianity alien to them, we expect that in a new land, where they would be in control, there would be freedom of conscience for all. But the new land provided only the opportunity for them to establish the kind of religiopolitical community that accorded with their convictions. Membership in the church was a precondition for citizenship in the community. Those who failed to qualify by their confession of faith for membership in the church were denied participation as citizens in the community. In other colonies, where Episcopalianism was in the saddle, there was a similar identification of church and state and a denial of freedom of worship to others than Episcopalians. In New York a Presbyterian missionary, Francis Makemie, was jailed for the offense of preaching a Presbyterian gospel and attempting to hold Presbyterian services of worship.

In fairness to those first Americans we must remember the context out of which they came. Not only in Britain but in all of Europe, religion and politics were everywhere mixed up together. A Catholic doctrine of the sovereignty of God over the whole of life was taken to mean the sovereignty of Catholicism and was used to justify Roman attempts to secure a Catholic political dominance in every land. Protestants had no difficulty in seeing the evil of that. But the same doctrine of the sovereignty of God was taken by Scottish Presbyterians to imply the sovereignty of a Presbyterian order of life and to justify even their attempt with an army to establish a Presbyterian government in London and a Presbyterian church in the whole of Britain. Each church, confident that it possessed the whole, or something very near the whole, of God's truth, was reluctant that there should be anyone in the realm without the benefit of such infallible guidance and direction for his or her life. These were the years when such religious arrogance in Europe and Britain, stemming largely from a doctrine of an infallible Scripture in which the infallibility was rather carelessly transferred from the Scriptures to each group's interpretation of Scripture, set Christian at war with Christian and devastated country after country. In America there were no such atrocities as that. But there was religious tyranny and religious oppression, and in time these generated a determination in varied sections of the population that in this new land there should be freedom for every person to worship and serve God according to his own conscience. This bore fruit when the nation was constituted. There was an insistence that all such misuse of religious power should come to an end and that nowhere in the nation should there be any religious establishment that would deny to others the free exercise of their religious convictions.

The denial of any religious establishment was not intended originally as the drawing of a sharp line between religion and politics, between sacred and secular realms. But only too often since then it has been interpreted as an absolute wall of separation between church and state, which then, as we have seen, creates a religious vacuum in the public, secular realm that in turn encourages the development of a state religion. Ironically, as that state religion captures the hearts of the citizens and acquires the authority of being the only authentic patriotic stance of a citizen, it takes on something of the character of a religious establishment which, at least psychologically, coerces the assent of many, in violation of the Constitution. It is the responsibility of the churches to see to it that for their members no such vacuum exists, that the faith they profess in the church is the faith with which they face their problems and make their decisions as citizens. The Puritans were right in insisting that God and his gospel must be sovereign in the totality of our life and in refusing to draw any sharp line between the religious and the political sphere. Where they were wrong was in assuming their own possession of the whole of God's truth and therefore the whole of his authority, and in failing to make room in their community for differing interpretations of the will of God. It is strange that the seventeenth century, when there were so many Protestant communities, each differing from the others in spite of all that they had in common, and all so earnest about possessing the truth, did not produce more persons who would have begun to suspect the limits of their own understanding and the possibility that at least at some points they might be wrong and others might be right.

The Scriptures as the only rule of faith and life were necessarily for these earliest Americans the basis of their definition of citizenship. And because they interpreted Scripture in a literalistic fashion, they tended to make of it a lawbook for the regulation of all things in life, somewhat after the fashion of the rabbis of pre-Christian Judaism. In fairness to the Puritans, however, we should speak first of how they lived out of the Scriptures in the most intense way, nourishing their minds and hearts daily on what they found there. They identified themselves readily with the Israel of the Old Testament. Their journey from Britain or Continental Europe was parallel with Israel's deliverance from the bondage of Egypt. Their landing in America was parallel with Israel's settlement in the Promised Land. They found the problems of the journey and of life in the new land reflected everywhere in the story of Israel, and not just the problems but also the answers to the problems, so that the Book for them was no mere chronicle of ancient events but was their guidebook for present journeying. The psalms that Israelites sang to keep up their courage on their long and dangerous journey through the centuries were the songs that kept the Puritan faith fresh and vital. And the Kingdom that the prophets of Israel saw so clearly before them as the goal of their journeying was the kingdom they were determined to establish on the new continent. The hope of its realization was what kept them alive in their most desperate trials.

There was another side, however, to their use of Scripture that is a warning to us of how *not* to use it for the definition of our citizenship. In their literalism they seized on texts and incidents in isolation, failing to bring them to the test of that center of Scripture in the light of which all texts are to be understood if the interpretation is to be Christian. That center is the Word incarnate in Jesus Christ and above all in his death and resurrection. The new American community, with Indians on its border threatening its life, found the Old Testament command of Yahweh for Israelites to destroy the Amalekites more congenial than either that other Old Testament command of Yahweh to deal kindly with the stranger within one's gates or the New Testament command of Jesus for his disciples to love their enemies. A superstitious fear of witches drew nourishment from Biblical condemnations of witchcraft, so that eventually in Salem Biblical guidance was responsible for one of the most disgraceful episodes in New England history, the hanging of "witches." Literalism revived the old Jewish Sabbath law, applied it to the Christian Sunday, and devised regulations that would have set Jesus himself in the stocks had he lived in seventeenth-century America. The New England experience should have been sufficient to demonstrate for all time that the Bible is not to be used as a lawbook out of which one extracts a pattern of Christian life that can be applied to all situations and made authoritative in any and every community.

How the Scriptures Are to Be Interpreted

We have a large and difficult task on our hands if we take seriously what is involved in finding in the Scriptures the authoritative basis for our life as citizens in the community. The Scriptures are a highly complex library of ancient writings that come to us from a succession of ages far distant and different from our own, a million words in sixty-six books of widely different character: prophetic sermons, histories quite unlike any modern histories, folktales, a hymnbook, apostolic letters, gospels—writings produced at various times and in various circumstances over a period of a thousand years in the life of a tiny nation called Israel on the eastern shore of the Mediterranean.

But we are citizens in a vastly different world today, a world that knows little and cares less about what ancient Hebrews thought, a world of airplanes, skyscrapers, computers, and hydrogen bombs, where television lets everyone know what everyone else is doing, and where those who have technology can have almost everything and those who lack it have less and less until they have almost nothing. One can well understand the skepticism with which many enlightened twentieth-century minds, both outside and inside the church, greet the claim that these random ancient Hebrew and Jewish records are the source out of which we as Christians must define everything that has to do with our life—our belief in God, our understanding of ourselves and of our relationships with others, our attitude toward the world and history, and the character of our conduct day by day.

Why should a first-century Near Eastern religious movement, with its roots in Hebrew religion and with a Palestinian carpenter as its central figure, exercise such an authority over us and, through the writings in which it defined itself, define also our life in the modern world? To that we can only answer that it is a mystery, has always been and will always be a mystery, a wonder, an oddity—but also a reality, that in this collection of widely different writings we have the absolutely unique once-and-for-all witness to what God has done, is doing, and yet means to do with us human beings in this world of his. In the fragment of history disclosed to us here, we have the essential clue to the meaning of all history, our nations' histories and our own individual histories. A light shines here that takes away the darkness of our world. In that light alone do we know who God is and who we are. In that light alone do we really begin to see the face of our neighbor.

In P. T. Forsyth's *Theology in Church and State* there is a passage on how to listen to Scripture that exposes graphically the error of literalism. The Bible, Forsyth says, is witness to the reality not just of God's truth but of God himself in much the same way that a score in music is the key not just to a succession of musical notes but to a whole world of beauty in the music of a great composer. The literalist spells out the words of Scripture just as anyone who can read a score can sound out the notes of the music. But the musician who would let the music of the great composers be heard must penetrate through the notes to the mind and spirit that first set them down as witness to the music he was hearing. Beethoven, according to his biographer, was comparatively careless about all the right notes of his music being played but was angry at once at any failure in expression or nuance or in apprehension of the character of the piece as a whole.

This principle, that each statement of a Biblical author must be understood first in the context of the total writings of that author and then in the larger context of the Scriptures as a whole, marks a significant development in contemporary Biblical scholarship. Historical criticism until recently tended to emphasize only the narrower context, as though each author existed in isolation, but Biblical theology has been rediscovering larger unities in each of the Testaments and in Scripture as a whole. Two American scholars have made important contributions to this development, John Bright in his *The Authority of the Old Testament* and Brevard Childs in the latter half of his *Biblical Theology in Crisis* and in his pioneering commentary on the book of Exodus. Both insist that the total canon of Scripture represents the context within which each text is to be interpreted. Not just the immediate historical situation but what preceded and what followed, what fed into the text and what grew out of the text, are essential to the understanding of the text itself. We do not rightly hear Jeremiah until we hear him together with Jesus, in whom his hopes for humanity were fulfilled. We do not rightly understand the content of the Creation stories in Genesis until we place them together with the stories of God's new creation in Jesus Christ. The Ninety-first Psalm will mislead us into a false conception of God's providence and protection unless we hear it together with the second temptation of Jesus, in which the devil quotes the psalm to encourage Jesus in a reckless expectation of God's help.

The Old Testament without the New is certain to have less than a Christian meaning. As Paul says in II Cor., ch. 3, there is a veil over the face of Moses (by which he means the Old Testament) until the crucified and risen Lord endows us with his Spirit and gives us eyes to see. But equally true is it that the New Testament without the Old loses its depth of meaning. To cut it apart from the Old is to separate it from its roots. The Old Testament as the sacred Scriptures of Jesus and of all the first Christians belonged to the very substance of their lives. They took for granted much of its content. They cannot be understood divorced from it. In fact, when we divorce them from it we inevitably give their words a different meaning from the one they intended. The title "Christ" applied to Jesus loses its meaning when it is forgotten that Jesus and Paul stand consciously in line with the prophets of Israel as the fulfillment of the promise inherent in their understanding of God's purpose for Israel—and through Israel for the world. This is a large and important subject, but it is sufficient for the present purpose merely to emphasize that fragments of Scripture dare not be torn out of their full canonical context and treated as though in themselves they were a full and sufficient revelation of God's counsel when they may express only a single aspect of the truth.

The importance of this principle becomes evident as soon as we begin to examine how Scripture has been used in defining Christian citizenship. There are three conspicuous breaches of the principle that have been operative in creating the unsatisfactory situation that confronts us in the churches.

The first misuse is the practice both in Germany and in

America among Protestants of isolating Rom., ch. 13, as though it were the first and the last word in Scripture concerning the relationship of the Christian to the civil government: "Let every person be subject to the governing authorities. For there is no authority except from God, and those that exist have been instituted by God. Therefore he who resists the authorities resists what God has appointed." Paul there is speaking not just of the Roman government but of all legally constituted governments. As the guardians of the security and welfare of every citizen, they are one aspect of God's providence. They set a restraint upon the powers of evil that unchecked would destroy the possibility of any kind of human life. Even in their imperfection they deserve the loyalty, gratitude, and obedience of all. But the New Testament has something more than that to say about the Roman government, and by implication about all governments. In Rev., ch. 13, Rome has become the beast out of the abyss that makes war against God's saints, sets itself upon the throne of God, and must be conquered if God is to establish his rule. Behind the first text we have Paul the Roman citizen, protected again and again by his Roman citizenship as he travels about the Empire, grateful for the order in the Roman world that gives him opportunity to preach his gospel and found his churches. But behind the second text we have a Christian church that has begun to disturb the Roman authorities and to be under suspicion of being a subversive force. As a result it has found in the civil government a cruel and heartless enemy bent upon its extermination.

These, however, are not the only texts that are relevant. In the Old Testament there are governments that are regarded as instituted by God and that have God's blessing. The ruler is called to his task by God and is promised God's support. Resistance to his rule is regarded as resistance to God. But there are other governments in Israel that are condemned as being in defiance of God, on which prophets pronounce God's judgment and rejection. Always in Israel human authority is prevented from becoming absolute, as happened in so many other Near Eastern lands, by the insistence that Yahweh is king of the universe and that the loyalty of the citizen is first and foremost to him. David at the height of his power has alongside him the prophet Nathan, not just to assure him of divine support but also to scourge him with God's judgment when his conduct is subversive of the supremacy of God's righteousness in Israel. Nathan, standing before such a powerful king as David and speaking the truth to him at the risk of his life, suggests something very different from submissiveness in political relationships and has to be taken seriously by Christians as a suggestion of how they may be most faithful in their citizenship.

Even more radical is what appears in the example of the prophet Ahijah. Under Solomon the government in Israel took on more and more the character of a dictatorship, the king's interests and needs absorbing most of the wealth of the nation and the sturdy independent citizens being reduced to a level little better than slavery. Solomon's successor made the situation worse. In protest the prophet Ahijah took the lead in a rebellion of the northern tribes against the authority of Jerusalem. At other times this prophetic intervention in politics could take a more positive form. Isaiah did not hesitate to offer his advice on foreign policy to the king. Jeremiah took the risk of being called a traitor when in a time of siege he advocated a policy of surrender to the Babylonians. He could see that resistance would mean only a useless starvation and slaughter of the civilian population, ending eventually in capitulation.

There were prophets and priests in Israel who found it more congenial and more profitable to equate the will of their king with the will of the unseen King, Yahweh. At one point, when the kings of Israel and Judah planned a joint expedition against some territory of the king of Syria, there were about four hundred prophets ready to tell their kings what they wanted to hear, and only one prophet, Micaiah, who saw a contradiction between the aggressive policy of his king and the will of Yahweh. Both Israelite regimes had to endure the constant presence in their midst of prophets who as spokesmen of the unseen King claimed authority over the life of the community superior to that of any earthly king. There was no confining of their interest to what happened in the shrines or in the soul life of Israelites. The concern of their God, and therefore their concern, was with the treatment of the poor in the marketplace, the quality of justice in the law courts, the protection of the little people against the ruthless ambitions of the wealthy and powerful, and the understanding by Israelites in general of their unique destiny as a people in covenant with a God of justice, compassion, and truth. Such a God expected of his people that his nature would be reflected in them in a justice, mercy, and integrity like his own. When Jesus said to his disciples, "Be like God," he was in direct line with the Old Testament prophets' conception of Israel's destiny, and ultimately of all mankind's. That Jesus should have narrowed the scope of Yahweh's concern to the "inner life" of his people is unthinkable and untrue to the New Testament record.

Paul's words in Rom., ch. 13, therefore, must be placed in their full canonical context. Taken alone and in isolation they seem to call for a completely passive submissiveness on the part of Christians in relation to whatever government may be in power. Understood in that sense, the words have been music in the ears of countless defenders of the established order. Representatives of government have drawn from them the assurance that they have God on their side when they have beaten down every movement of protest against their policies. Kings and queens of the sixteenth and seventeenth centuries in Britain and elsewhere no doubt comforted themselves with those words of Paul when they sent Christians to prison or burned them at the stake for no other offense than disagreeing with government policy. The Reformers themselves set a bad example in this regard. Martin Luther would have Rom., ch. 13, in mind when he encouraged the princes in a ruthless suppression of the Peasants' Revolt. So also would Zwingli when he permitted the Zurich city council to drown the recalcitrant Anabaptists in the lake, and Calvin when he got rid of the Geneva prostitutes by having some of them disposed of in the same manner.

But we do not have to look back so far in history for illustrations of the misuse of Rom., ch. 13. Would the Nazi program have gone on so long unchallenged by the churches and would six million Jews have died if Rom., ch. 13, had been balanced with Rev., ch. 13 and the prophets of Israel? Would there have been the same reluctance of American Christians to criticize their government's program in Vietnam if the prophets of the Old Testament had been more to the fore in shaping the preaching and the contents of church school teaching in the American churches? How can Christians stand by silent, with no word of criticism or rebuke, while their governments institute policies that bring suffering and ruin upon millions of human beings? And standing by silent, mind you, with a good conscience because of Rom., ch. 13 ! Paul, were he living today, would be aghast that his words should have been used to keep the church silent and inactive in the face of such devastating evils.

A second misuse of Scripture through the isolation of individual texts in order to limit the scope of Christian concern is to be found in a common misinterpretation of two sayings of Jesus. One, "Give to Caesar what is Caesar's and to God what is God's," seems quite clearly to make a sharp division between the secular and the religious realm. In the secular realm the citizens owe allegiance to the state and only in the religious realm does God claim their obedience. So also in Jesus' words, "My kingdom is not of this world," there seems to be a clear distinction between a this-worldly and an other-worldly realm. Jesus thus claims authority over men's souls but leaves to the civil government the ordering of their life in the external world. Caesar holds sway in the political realm while God holds sway in the spiritual realm! But is this customary interpretation valid?

Both these texts require closer examination. The first was spoken in a situation where Jesus' enemies were attempting to get him into trouble either with the Roman authorities or with his own Jewish fellow citizens. They asked him whether God's law as he understood it commanded Jews to pay taxes to the Romans. If he said it did, then his fellow countrymen, who hated the Roman taxes as the extortions of an alien army of occupation, would turn against him. If he said it did not, they had only to report his answer to the Roman authorities to have them brand him a rebel who was encouraging revolt. Jesus' response was a masterpiece of prophetic cunning. He called for a Roman coin and, pointing to the face of Caesar on it, gave his answer: "Give to Caesar what is Caesar's and to God what is God's."

By the first part of that answer Jesus was certainly refusing to let himself be classified as a rebel against the Roman rule. S. G. F. Brandon's attempt, in his book *Jesus and the Zealots,* to prove that Jesus was in sympathy with the revolutionary party, the Zealots, who advocated a violent expulsion of the Romans, is not at all convincing. In Jesus' temptations, before ever he began his mission, he had distinguished clearly between a form of messiahship that would attempt to establish God's rule by force, by seizing the political power, and a messiahship that would take the "servant" route, working from beneath to transform the relationships that give human society its character. From the first moment of his public work Jesus was the servant Messiah, which even his most devoted disciples found very hard to understand.

The second half of the answer has a sting concealed in it that may be missed by us when we have only the bare words but would not be missed by the group of men whose hostility to Jesus was due to their resentment of the exorbitant claim he made upon them in the name of God. Jesus' critique of contemporary Jewish religion was that in its legalistic defining of what God expected of men and women it let them off too easily. By their keeping of set rules and by their fasting and almsgiving they could give themselves a good conscience before God when actually they were withholding from him what he asked before all else—the surrender of themselves to be open to him in faith, open also to their neighbor's need, and willing unconditionally to be at God's disposal to get on with his redemption of the world. The power of faith for Jesus was in the totality of man's surrender to God. These men who were trying to entrap him knew no such power of faith. They were religious without faith. Their corruption in mind and heart was that they would not give to God what belonged to God.

Only when we re-create the situation and recognize these personal factors in the confrontation between Jesus and his enemies do we give to Jesus' words their original significance. Jesus struck at the heart of the spiritual paralysis of these men when he said to them: "Yes! By all means give Caesar his taxes but, much more important, give to God the place in your life that he claims from you." Every Jew knew what God claimed. He heard it every time he heard the Shema: "Hear, O Israel." Jesus was no innovator in this. God claimed the love and obedience of his people in every department of their life. An Israel responding to God's love with love would be an Israel shining as a light in all the world. Therefore Jesus' words on this occasion, understood in their immediate context and in their larger canonical context, cannot be construed as drawing a line between the political and the religious area of life and narrowing his interest and concern to a purely religious sphere.

With the second saying of Jesus, "My kingdom is not of this world," one has to cut it apart from its immediate context in order to give it an otherworldly meaning. Jesus is explaining why his disciples do not fight against his arrest. His kingdom is not the kind of worldly rule in which men fight with weapons to assert their power. His power is a different kind of power, not an external compulsion on anyone to do anything, not an ability to prevent his own arrest and crucifixion, but a strange kind of power that he would continue to exercise through the centuries from his cross. Jesus always had trouble getting people to understand what he meant by the kingdom. It was not a shadowy spiritual realm somewhere beyond this world or, as Tolstoy suggested, in the inner life of persons. Jesus told his disciples to pray, "Thy kingdom come, Thy will be done on earth as it is in heaven." That means here and now in this world. It is a new order of life, a new kind of humanity, a humanity that has been purged of its inhumanity by the transforming presence and power of a living God, invading this world now with profound consequences in every department of life, certainly not excluding the political and the economic, which are so determinative of the quality of human life. The quotation from Isa., ch. 61, with which Jesus began his first sermon in his hometown synagogue shows the direction in which his interest lay: "Good news to the poor" means bread for the hungry and homes for the homeless. That is economics. "Release for the captives and liberty for the oppressed" means an end to injustice in the community. That is politics. Jesus' kingdom is not an otherworldly kingdom that lets his followers dream of an ideal order somewhere beyond the present world and beyond the present time while they turn their backs on the urgent social, economic, and political dilemmas of the world community in which they have their present life.

What Jesus Meant by "Salvation"

A third and very common misuse of Scripture through an ignoring of the canonical context is the misinterpretation of the words "salvation" and "saved." They are now very generally taken to refer almost exclusively to an inner spiritual conversion by which a person becomes a Christian and receives assurance of eternal life. Even more narrowly the question, "Are you saved?" has come to have the meaning usually, "Have you been converted and made a public confession of faith at an evangelistic service?"

The words have a wide range of meaning in the Scriptures. In the Old Testament it is the whole community rather than individuals that experience salvation or for which salvation is hoped. The great decisive saving event is the deliverance from Egypt, which then becomes the model of future deliverances. In Second Isaiah "salvation" is one of the words used to describe the perfect order of justice and righteousness that will comprehend the life of all the nations when God through Israel his servant will have established his rule on earth and every knee bows to him in obedience. It and its synonym "righteousness" are very close in meaning to "Kingdom of God" in Jesus' teaching. When in the Psalms it is used of individuals it usually describes not a spiritual experience in which they are reconciled with God but rather some deliverance from sickness or peril or oppression or death. In the New Testament the dawning of the day of salvation is the coming of the day when Israel's destiny will be fulfilled. The song of Zechariah at the birth of John the Baptist anticipates a salvation in which Israel will be saved from all its enemies and God's forgiveness of past sins will be the prelude to a glorious future. The interpretation of Jesus' name in Matt. 1:21, "for he will save his people from their sins," has this national rather than an individual connotation. The "salvation" that Simeon rejoices to have seen in Luke 2:30 is plainly the new day heralded by Second Isaiah when Israel was to become "a light to the nations." Parallel with this is Mary's expectation in the Magnificat of a great reversal of fortunes in which the high and mighty are brought low and God's poor see the fulfillment of all their hopes.

Jesus' proclamation of the coming of the Kingdom is his announcement that the salvation heralded by the prophets, and most recently by John the Baptist, is not just a future prospect but a fulfillment of life that is possible in the present moment. The hour of decision has struck. No one need wait any longer. Where there is openness and a readiness to respond, a new life, and with that new life a new world, can begin. Jesus knew in himself that possibility, and not just possibility but the joyful reality of a true humanity through the indwelling of God's Spirit, and his mission was to open the door to that life first to Israel and then beyond Israel and through a restored Israel to all mankind.

It is significant that Jesus uses the words "salvation" and "saved" so infrequently, much less frequently than Paul. He prefers to speak of the Kingdom of God or the Kingdom of Heaven, which emphasizes the communal nature of the salvation and links it definitely with the prophetic hope for the future. When he describes his mission as "to seek and to save the lost," the "lost" is not a synonym for the "damned" but rather refers to the whole range of Israelites who for various reasons found themselves excluded from the ordinances of the Jewish faith. No one any longer cared what happened to them. Tax collectors, lawbreakers, and undoubtedly many who had just drifted away from the strict order of the synagogue community, belonged in this category. They were lost to the Israel of faith, and Jesus, alienated by the self-righteousness that was the besetting sin of the members of the synagogue, made these outsiders the special objects of his mission. He met with a readier response to his good news from them than from the more respectable people in the synagogue. "Saving" them meant rescuing them from their present life, in which they were divorced from spiritual resources (exclusion from the synagogue would be interpreted by a first-century Jew as exclusion from God), and opening to them the present possibility of life in God's Kingdom and in the fellowship of those who belonged within the Kingdom. When Jesus said to those who responded to his gospel with repentance and faith, "Your faith has saved you," it had this full meaning.

Paul prefers to speak of "salvation" where Jesus would speak of "the Kingdom." Both terms describe the same reality. A third parallel term is "life" or "eternal life," which is used by the author of the Fourth Gospel in preference to both "Kingdom" and "salvation." One can understand the abandonment of the term "Kingdom of God" by those who were interpreting Jesus' gospel to a Gentile world. The "kingdom" had a rich Hebrew background that was still vividly alive in the Jewish community addressed by Jesus, but it would be much less meaningful, if not completely strange, for Gentiles. The words "salvation" and "life," however, were universally meaningful. All three terms had both present and future significance: the kingdom coming now, yet still to come in its fullness; life now in the power of the Spirit that by its very nature as life in God is life eternal; salvation, which is a present deliverance out of the tyranny of sin and into the life of grace, but which does not reach its fullness in time until it comprehends the whole creation—or in eternity until God completes our redemption. Salvation for Paul as for Jesus is both present and future. It can never be looked back upon as something finished in the past. For a Christian to say, "I have been saved," as though the event were complete, would be to lose one whole essential dimension of New Testament salvation. Jesus plants the seed of the word in the human soil, but the flowering of it belongs to the future. Paul at the very end of his life insists that he has not yet achieved his goal. Salvation is nearer than when he first believed, but he strains forward, pressing toward the mark, trusting the promise that God will finish the work that he has begun in him.

Also for Paul, as for the prophets of the Old Testament, salvation must take in the whole creation. It is nothing less than a new creation with new relationships, not just between God and man and between human beings but also between human beings and their environment in nature. The whole creation groans and travails, he says in Rom., ch. 8, waiting for liberation from its bondage to decay. Certainly such a liberation as that would mean the liberation of human beings from the economic and political structures that hold them in a condition of slavery and starvation.

Against this background we begin to realize how narrow and inadequate it is to regard the word "salvation" in the Scriptures as referring exclusively or even primarily to a sudden experience of conversion. That may be an essential part of it for some persons, as it was for Paul, but it should be only a part of it. Yet it is likely that 99 percent of persons, both inside and outside the church, when they hear the words "salvation" and "saved," think at once of the kind of conversion experience that takes place usually in the setting of an evangelistic service. Then, when they are told that, while the prophets of the Old Testament may have busied themselves with problems of justice and right relations in the economic and political realms, Jesus confined his mission exclusively to the saving of souls, the whole weight of Biblical authority is used perversely to warn present-day ministers, and the church in general, away from any concern with what is happening in the realm of public life.

We need to look more carefully at this phrase, "the saving of souls," which has had a long currency in the church. It is not to be found anywhere in the Scriptures. It embodies a conception of persons that is totally alien to Biblical ways of thinking. The idea of a soul that resides somewhere in the body but is to be distinguished sharply from the body has its origin not in Israel but in Greece. For the Greeks the body was a prison house for the soul, but for the Hebrews the body was part of God's good creation. Human beings in body, mind, and heart were selves, persons, intended by God to reflect his nature in their total being. The Greek separation between soul and body has been shown by modern investigations to be both bad physiology and bad psychology. The body with all its actions and its passions is an integral part of the self. Moreover, the self is a unity in its inner experiences and its outward actions. We do not know who we are until we look with open eyes at what we have done. And there is no genuine salvation as an inner experience without a corresponding transformation of the outward conduct. And the outward conduct includes our attitudes and actions in the social, economic, political, and cultural spheres of our life.

This criticism of language about "saving souls" should not suggest any disparagement of the converting function of the gospel. Preaching and teaching that does not aim to convert, that does not aim to produce a transformation in the character and quality of life, is not Christian. The word of God is not ever to be heard by us, really heard, without bringing us under God's judgment and inducing in us a change of mind and heart. But when the word that saves souls is set in antithesis to the word of the prophets, which rebuked public wrong and in God's name tried to save the community from its sins, a serious and debilitating perversion of the New Testament gospel has set in.

We may well ask how a Greek conception of the soul has come to have such wide currency among Christians, embodying as it does an idea of the human person that is at odds with what we find in both Testaments. Our Western civilization is far more Greek than Hebrew. One has only to think of how until recently education in the Western world was based on the Greek and Roman literature. The Enlightenment in the eighteenth century, which largely shaped the thinking of the modern world, was enraptured with Greek ideas and frequently hostile to the Biblical tradition. But, added to this, there has been the influence of the King James version of the Scriptures, which constantly uses the term "soul," where the Hebrew and the Greek demand a word that would be less compromised and would indicate the whole person. If the King James version is compared with any competent modern version, it is striking how frequently the word "soul" disappears. A third and strongly influential factor has been the evangelistic tradition, which has played such a large part in the shaping of the North American churches and still dictates in wide areas their language and thought forms. We need, therefore, to recover the full canonical context of these words "salvation" and "saved" and to trace out their meaning in an adequate modern translation. Their liberation from a long imprisonment in a too narrow context could be a liberation for many Christians and for many churches.

IN THE LIGHT OF THE CROSS

The final test of these interpretations of Scripture is how they appear in the light of the cross. If the decisive word on the believer's relation to the civil authorities is to be Rom., ch. 13, alone, then not only were the prophets misinterpreters of God's will but Jesus' defiance of the legally constituted authorities in his community was wrong both when he interfered in the regulation of the Temple courts and when he refused obedience to the food and Sabbath laws. We dare not forget that his forceful expulsion of the money changers was an illegal act, just as illegal and as infuriating to the governing powers as Father Philip Berrigan's pouring of blood on Selective Service files in Baltimore. If Christian citizenship means unvarying obedience to the civil authorities without regard to the character of their rule, then Jesus could not qualify as a Christian citizen and we would have to pronounce both the Roman and the Jewish officials justified in the act of crucifixion, since to them he was clearly a lawbreaker and a dangerously subversive influence in the community—not at all the kind of citizen who was to be encouraged.

The cross has become to such a degree a *religious* symbol and is placed so consistently at the center of the religious ritual that we may easily forget that it represents a political confrontation. It was a political act not only by the Sanhedrin and by Pilate but also by Jesus. The authorities felt themselves sufficiently affronted and threatened by Jesus' words and actions that they wanted to get rid of him. What impelled Judas, a committed disciple, one of the twelve chosen by Jesus to share the work and the abuse of his mission with him, a trained evangelist who had given up everything for this venture, suddenly to change in his loyalty and betray him to the civil authorities? There is no other reasonable explanation than that as a loyal citizen of Judah he became aware that, if Jesus had his way, the whole existing structure of Judean life would be shattered. The political implications of Jesus' mission frightened Judas, and more than Judas. One has only to think of how they frightened and angered another deeply loyal and deeply earnest Jew, Paul. Jesus was not content with changing the lives of individuals. His journey to the national capital, Jerusalem, focused attention on what he purposed for the nation as a whole. The aim of his mission was nothing less than a transformation in the character of Israel. The cross was a political device that was meant by the authorities to preserve the *status quo*.

The third misinterpretation that portrays Jesus as an itinerant evangelist with no other interest than the saving of individual souls from hell and damnation fails to grasp the larger focus of Jesus' mission on Israel as the covenant people of God, destined through the ages to be eventually the servant of his redemptive purpose for the whole world. Detaching Jesus from the prophets and from the Old Testament makes it easy to fall into this misrepresentation of him. The tragedy of Israel in Jesus' day which he saw so clearly was that the wider vision had been largely lost. The most earnest religious people in the nation, conscious of the superiority of their Jewish religion in comparison with that of other nations, had become content to guard its purity and had little interest in the mediation of a knowledge of God to the Gentile world. The most forceful spokesman for that world vision had been the nameless prophet in Isa. chs. 35; 40 to 66, who expected it to be fulfilled in two stages, first an ingathering and reconstitution of the nation and then an outreach to all the nations of the world (ch. 49:5, 6). Jesus' use of that prophet's words to depict his own mission and his use of the "Servant" image for his own and his disciples' calling suggests a similar breadth in his intention and that his focus upon "the lost sheep of the house of Israel" represented only the first stage in a mission that as it continued would reach out far beyond the borders of the house of Israel. His call not just to individuals within Israel but to Israel as a whole is what explains why he cut short his ministry in Galilee and took the road to Jerusalem. He had to confront the nation at its center in order to fulfill his primary purpose.

If the sole purpose of Jesus' ministry was the saving of individual souls, then his journey to Jerusalem, which plunged him knowingly into a dangerous situation, was an irresponsible provocative act. If he had stayed away from

Jerusalem, he could have gone on for many years saving souls. It is unlikely that anyone would have become frightened about the intentions of such an evangelist. Judas would have spent his life happily and productively as one of the assistant evangelists. It was only when the political implications of Jesus' ministry and teachings became evident in Jerusalem that opposition to him suddenly hardened and his crucifixion became inevitable.

Still today, as long as the church confines its attention to evangelism, to the spiritual welfare and the inner life of persons, it rarely gets into any trouble. In fact, at the present moment, that seems to be the surefire recipe for a successful church. It is when conversions begin to take place in the outer life, the public life, the political, economic and social life of Christians, that the church becomes a thorn in the side of the community—and thereby a leaven of change, an instrument of God's enlightening judgment and the servant of his wider redemption. If we limit ourselves to saving souls, we are not likely ever to face the possibility of crucifixion. Rather, an affluent society such as ours seems more inclined to reward us liberally for setting such a judicious limitation upon our Christianity.

3

The Biblical Perspective

Our exploration of the Biblical basis of citizenship thus far has had a predominantly negative or critical character. It was essential to expose the fragmentary use of Scripture and the misinterpretations that result in a politically irresponsible church, creating a religious vacuum in public life conducive to the growth of a state religion. An authoritative Bible (and it is still authoritative for a high percentage of church people), wrongly interpreted, can have disastrous social and political consequences. It can also disrupt the life of whole denominations. For their own good and for the public good our churches should give more attention to the development of sound hermeneutical principles both in the training of ministers in the seminaries and in the educational programs of local congregations.

Millions of Bibles each year are scattered across the land, but the most elementary principles for understanding them unfortunately remain unknown even to people who worship regularly in the churches. The idea apparently is widespread that the Bible really needs no interpretation, that it has only to be opened and read to give forth its message. Were that true there would be no need for a church. An agency for the distribution of Bibles would be sufficient. But Jesus did not entrust his gospel to a written text. He entrusted it to a community of disciples who, indwelt by his Spirit, would by their word and action be the interpreters of his gospel. The

71

Bible demands alongside it a responsible interpreting church, a church that constantly lets its mind and heart and daily life be shaped by what it hears from the Scriptures. It is only in such a church that the implications of a Biblical faith for present-day citizenship are likely to be spelled out with any clarity or effectiveness. We must now attempt in some measure to fulfill that constructive task.

It would be misleading, however, if here at the beginning the impression were created that Christians have only to consult the Scriptures to find all the answers to the problems that confront them as citizens. There is an old saying, none the less true for being old, that he who knows only the Scriptures is unable to understand the Scriptures. The voice that speaks to us through the Scriptures addresses us where we are and as we are. But who, what, and where we are, in our personal, social, political, and economic existence, we need to learn from the most dependable sources of our own time—from newspapers, journals and books, and our own careful observation. Our world, our civilization, our communities, our selves are the product of a variety of past and present forces. Our Western civilization, which provides the general framework of our life, stems as much from Greece and Rome as from Palestine, if not more. As we shall later see, that furnishes us with some of our most acute problems. The wisdom of Greece and the wisdom of Palestine have their points of conflict.

Also we had best recognize that not all the wise men of the past have been Christians, nor are all the wise men of the present Christians. We owe a colossal debt to Greece in science, art, literature, and philosophy, and to Rome in law and government. But if Greece and Rome determine our basic understanding of ourselves, our world, our God, then as Christians we are hopelessly confused. That influence reaches our modern world by way of the Enlightenment of the eighteenth century, which in many of its spokesmen was scornful of both Christian and Jewish traditions, but insofar as it set men thinking critically, questioning everything that had formerly been taken for granted, it had far-reaching consequences for the Christian church. It opened new channels of investigation both in the interpretation of Scripture and in theological thinking in general. Today much of the ferment in religion which we are experiencing is simply that after two centuries the Enlightenment movement has finally broken through to the man in the street and the teen-ager in the school. They are distrustful of all traditions. They want to see and know for themselves. They are no longer willing to be treated as children by the church. Then there is the whole technological development of our century, complicating everything, creating wholly new situations and new problems (e.g., the complexities both economic and political resulting from the mushrooming multinational corporations in the last ten years), reducing the power of the individual and multiplying many times over the power of government.

As citizens we need to know the nature of the world in which we live and in which we make our decisions. But if we are to be *Christian* citizens, it is essential that in the midst of this complex world we hear with clarity the voice of Scripture and learn to distinguish it from all the other voices that are constantly ringing in our ears, for we have not only to hear it but to let it become our voice with real integrity (for *we* are the interpreting church), that through us it may command a hearing and exert its influence upon the shaping of our world. Passive Christians who are content merely to hear are inadequate. The hearing of faith, to be a genuine hearing, truly creative, must issue in present word and action. The real hermeneutical problem, insufficiently recognized and dealt with in seminaries, is how, for the layman in his use of the Scriptures, the gap is to be bridged not just between ancient and present meaning but, one stage farther, between the layman's hearing and his translation of what he hears into what he says and does in the situations of everyday life.

The Centrality of the Cross

We have already used the cross as a test of certain interpretations of Jesus' words. It must eventually be the testing place of whatever we put forward as Christian citizenship. One of the strange things about the Christian gospel is the way in which all of its meaning comes to a concentrated point in a man dying on a cross. What was intended to silence him forever quickly became the means of his most effective continuing proclamation. No one familiar with the New Testament would be likely to dispute that the cross, together with the resurrection, is central in every part of it, not only in the Gospels, where it occupies a wholly disproportionate space in comparison with the life and teachings of Jesus, but also in Paul's letters and in the remaining books. But many Christians might have difficulty in seeing what positive and constructive significance the cross has for the defining of their citizenship. The cross is to them a purely religious symbol, a church symbol, with significance for their inner spiritual life and unrelated to politics. They expect to see it in the chancels or on the steeples of churches. Worn on a chain around the neck, it is the mark of a very devout person, and sometimes of an official of the church. But in all these uses centuries of sentiment veil the actuality of the cross. Before all else it was the instrument of a political execution. The modern parallel would be a firing squad or a hangman's noose or an electric chair. We translate everything else in Scripture. Why not translate the cross? Would a congregation be shocked if, as they entered the church on Sunday, they found a hangman's noose at the center of the chancel instead of the cross? Yet, in the light of Dietrich Bonhoeffer's fate, that would be a translation into readily comprehensible twentieth-century terms. Much of the adulation of the cross rests upon a serious misunderstanding.

The connection between the cross and citizenship becomes clearer when we see, first, that it is only one of many crosses in the Biblical story, and then that all these crosses are the consequence of political implications in the words and actions of God's spokesmen. Elijah has to flee for his life from Queen Jezebel. Micaiah is thrown into prison for refusing to set the stamp of God's approval on a war that the kings of

Israel and Judah wanted to wage against Syria. Jeremiah had his own fellow townsmen conspiring against his life and later was left to die at the bottom of a deep well. John the Baptist had his head chopped off for challenging the moral conduct of the king. Paul five times received thirty-nine lashes, three times was beaten with rods, once was stoned and left for dead, and after years in prison was executed by the Romans.

These are only a few instances excerpted from a long Biblical succession. We are forced to ask, what is this all about? Why all these companions of the cross, before and after? Second Isaiah, the great theologian of the Old Testament, summed it all up when he drew the portrait of the Servant of the Word. His book, read with care, discloses what he and his followers in their day experienced as the price of faithfulness to their calling—scorn, hatred, beatings, insults in the street, expulsion from their community, and certainly for some it meant a pseudolegal condemnation and death. The prophet knew how frequently this had been the lot of his predecessors and, looking forward, he could see no other prospect for those who would follow in his footsteps. Therefore in ch. 53 of his book he faced unblinkingly the strange mystery that God seemed to have no other way to overcome the blindness and perverseness of mankind than to incarnate his truth so deeply in the lives of those who let themselves be bound to him in faith that his nature, reflected in them, became the means of a confrontation between God and his enemies. First the Servant in his faithfulness had to bear the agony of man's brutal rejection of God and of God's truth, but eventually God's word and Spirit in the Servant would reveal in the encounter their power to open blind eyes and to transform enemies into sons and servants.

We need to ask what all the crosses in Old and New Testament have in common. Their political character is evident at once. Elijah was the defender of the little people in Israel against a tyrannical king and queen who were trampling on them, defrauding them of their rights and corrupting their religious institutions. Micaiah took his life in his hands to oppose a war that for no good reason would cost the lives of many Israelites and exhaust the nation's resources. Jeremiah had a long record of criticizing the most popular religious and political policies of his day and of standing in the way of the realization of the current national ambition. It was when he called for surrender to the Babylonians during the siege of Jerusalem that he was branded a traitor and left in a well to die. John the Baptist was allowed his freedom as long as he confined his attention to converting and baptizing men and women; it was when he criticized the conduct of a political ruler that he lost his life.

The pre-Christian Paul helps us see how Jesus belongs in this succession. Why would such an earnest religious man as Paul want to stamp out every vestige of the movement begun by Jesus? It may look like religious fanaticism but we understand it only when we recognize how interwoven were civil and religious elements in the first-century Jewish community. Social, economic, political, and religious laws were all mingled together in the religious structure of Judaism. To challenge Torah was to endanger the national existence. Paul's devotion to Torah was automatically devotion to the national interest. And Jesus' undermining of Torah by his words and actions was a serious threat to the nation's future. Paul's own sufferings as a Christian apostle had the same origin. We sometimes forget that when he became a Christian he nevertheless remained a loyal and devoted member of the international Jewish community. He was both a Roman and a Jewish citizen. Therefore, since like Jesus he broke with the rule of Torah, his fellow Jews wherever he went accused him of treachery and of endangering the future of his nation. So bitter was the antagonism to him in Jerusalem that he would have been assassinated by the mob had he not been rescued by Roman soldiers.

In every instance these spokesmen for God, a grim succession that gives the Old and New Testaments striking unity, were punished by their communities for their conflict with what seemed most obviously to be the national interest. Because of their relationship with God these men, all of them, had a vision of the nation's destiny and a conception of their responsibility as citizens that was at odds with the accepted pattern and standard of good citizenship. Make no mistake, they were patriots, imbued with a love of their nation and a concern for its welfare so deep and passionate that no suffering heaped on them could make them deviate for a moment from the course that to them was essential to its future.

The cross, therefore, stands at the very beginning of our discussion as a warning that *Christian* citizenship is a difficult enterprise and may be a dangerous one. In it there can be no easy and comfortable conformity with established mores. Good citizenship in a democracy is often thought of as conformity with whatever policies and attitudes happen to have the approval of the majority, supporting whatever is generally agreed to be the national interest. In a dictatorship the conformity is enforced by penalties. But democracies have their unofficial penalties that even in ordinary times can be painful and in a time of national crisis can be severe. The Christian citizen, however, under the sign of the cross, has to recognize that he belongs in a tradition that makes him always look beyond what seems to be the immediate national interest. He cannot be an unquestioning nationalist. There is always a critical tension between his loyalty to his nation and his loyalty to his God. Love of his neighbor makes him willing to serve and, if need be, to sacrifice for his nation, but love of God and obedience to his God makes him always subordinate the national interest to God's interest, that is, to God's new order in the nation and beyond the nation in the world at large.

We are not usually aware how powerful are the forces of national interest and national loyalty in all of us. We have no reason to be ashamed of them. Like love of home and an intelligent love of self, they are essential to a healthy life. It is only when they become absolutes, taking precedence over all other considerations, that they compromise our Christian faith. But when that happens in us, we have demoted God to second place, which may still seem to be a very important place, in the order of our life, and nationalism in us has become a dangerous idolatry. There can be no idolatry of the nation in Christian citizenship. Under the sign of the cross one is forced constantly to look beyond the immediate situation, the established order, the national interest. The cross becomes the question mark that God's new world, incarnated in Jesus, sets against the present order of our world, no matter how agreeable to us that present order may chance to be.

GOD THE CREATOR

From the cross we draw a line back to the Creation story. Our understanding of God and of God's relationship with man determines the character of our citizenship. The prophets and Jesus and Paul were the troublesome progressive citizens that they were because they worshiped a Creator God whose will and purpose for his world transcended the will, the purpose, and the interests of any body of human beings, however great their power or impressive their wisdom. For them there was a *distance* between God and man. God was Creator and man was creature, beloved of God, his constant care, intended in nature to reflect God's own nature, yet in the unfolding of his life in society a rebel against God.

Basic to the Biblical story is this contradiction between the world of God's intention and the world as it actually existed at any given moment in history. The prophet who is so near to God is aghast that his highest thoughts and aspirations are so contrary to what he discusses concerning God's will for the human race. God is God and man is man. And in that distinction lies man's hope. The concept of the transcendence of God has been having a rough time in recent years. Scornful things have been written about a God who is "up there" or "out there," as though the distance the Biblical authors set between God and man, heaven and earth, were a distance in space. The result is usually to encourage an immanentalism in which the believer brings his God near by identifying him with some higher element in himself or in the world process. What is then lost is the Biblical awareness of the radical tension between God and man, between God's world and man's world, which is the dynamic that in the Biblical story, and beyond it, sets man endlessly in motion toward a distant goal in history. Always in the story, brooding over it, is the consciousness of a destiny that has been missed and of a transcendent, yet present, God who is not willing that that destiny should remain unfulfilled. And it is this tension between Creator and creature, between the divine and the human will, that creates the crosses, at the same time generating the power that drives man ever forward toward an as yet unrealized future. Without a transcendent God there would be no history moving toward a goal. There is a warning in that for us, that with the loss of faith in a transcendent Creator God, the Biblical God, human history has been deprived of its essential dynamic.

A UNIVERSAL PERSPECTIVE

The Creation stories establish a universal outlook which is maintained throughout both Testaments, though some participants, both Israelite and Christian, may have a narrower perspective. It is a rather curious Creator who meets us in both stories. In the first one, he brings a world into being just by speaking and in the second, earlier story he goes at the task of fashioning human beings with his hands. Also it is a curious world that he creates—just one continent, a kind of flat island floating on water and with oceans all around it— but it represents all that exists. Translated into modern terms, it is the vast universe disclosed to us by the astronomer's telescope and by the physicist's exploration of the atom. What is essential is that it all belongs to God and bears the marks of his design. The perspective in both stories is universal. The actors are not Hebrews or Egyptians or Babylonians but are the parents of all mankind. After the Flood, God makes a covenant with all the earth. The covenant which later he makes with Israel, promising to be their God in a special way and to give them a special destiny in human history, may seem at first to constitute a narrowing of that perspective, but that is to misunderstand it, a misunderstanding to which Israelites themselves were prone and which the prophets had consistently to correct. The covenant relation with Israel belonged within the universal covenant and concern and had as its purpose the eventual achievement of God's design for mankind. The Israelites, however, were prone, like all other nations, to identify God with their national interest, making him a supernatural support for their national ego and for the way of life that seemed to them essential for their continuance. Had there been no other Israel than that, there would be no Bible. The Bible exists because of a minority of citizens within the nation, sustained by a succession of prophets, which formed a center of continuing dissent and witness and maintained a world outlook. The main line of Biblical faith was sustained only by a minority rather than by the nation as a whole. The two outlooks stand in sharp contrast in The Book of Jonah, where an author who represents the universal perspective of the minority holds up to ridicule in the figure of Jonah the narrow, nationalistically oriented attitude of the majority in its utterly inhuman indifference about the fate of the Gentile world.

We Christians are likely to give ourselves high marks at this point. We identify at once with the prophets and with the Israelite minority, whose vision we see fulfilled in the Christian church. Here at least, we tell ourselves, we come up to the Biblical standard. One of the proudest achievements of our churches in the last two centuries has been the planting of the church on every continent and island. We have carried the gospel to the ends of the earth. Admittedly there are members of the church whose vision does not reach beyond the borders of their own land, or, for that matter, beyond the borders of their own immediate community and congregation, but as churches our outlook is universal. But what are the dimensions of the outlook of our church members *as citizens?* Religiously their interest is worldwide. But in their citizenship they are likely to think that their responsibility ends at their national boundary. It is notorious that members of missionary societies often confine their interest in what is happening to other nations to the communities where they have workers and rarely look beyond these "missions" to the larger problems of the societies in which the missions are located. It is a serious contradiction and inconsistency that Christians should have a world perspective religiously but only a national perspective politically, economically, and socially. The Creator God of the Scriptures, with the whole world and the whole of humanity as his concern, calls for a church in his own likeness and a Christian citizenship with the same breadth of concern.

In a time when modern technology is turning what once were distant continents into a single neighborhood and the demand of the hour is for persons who can think and act as world citizens, it is pathetic that a church founded on the Scriptures has not been more productive of what is needed. Nationalism in all our lands has been the shaping force in citizenship. We live in an era of passionate nationalisms. The idolatry of nationalism becomes conspicuous when in a Nazi order all concealment is thrown off and the national interest as the *summum bonum* demands total submission. It then becomes clear that the Creator God of the Scriptures and the people of that God, Jews and Christians alike, are the implacable antagonists of such idolatry. But when nationalism is less brutal, less obvious and more refined, when it is content with less visible forms of self-assertion and its harshness is softened by programs of international aid, it becomes possible for Christians to be unaware of the extent to which they are nationalists in their citizenship. Nationalism does not need to have bad manners. It does not have to be anti-Jewish or anti-Christian. In fact, it can dress itself up in many of the virtues of a Christian order and can even pose as the defender of that order. And it is possible for Christians to be captured by an idolatry of nation without even knowing that it has happened. We need to test ourselves because nationalism has become the number one temptation of twentieth-century Christians. Where are the boundaries of our interest and concern as citizens? Which symbol evokes the more passionate response from us, the flag or the cross? I suspect that in most churches the removal of the cross from the chancel would make people only wonder where it had gone and why, but the removal of the flag from the chancel would at once cause much more serious concern. Paul Minear in his book *I Pledge Allegiance* includes a letter in which a minister comments on how much more enthusiastically his people sing a national hymn than any other, merely Christian hymn. We are born most of us into both communities, church and national, and we grow up with the two allegiances interwoven without even stopping to ask ourselves which is primary and which is secondary. Not until we make a conscious decision is our God likely to have first place.

The biography by Townsend Hoopes, *The Devil and John Foster Dulles* (1973), illustrates vividly the far-reaching consequences of this inner conflict in a Christian in public office. Dulles came of a strong Christian tradition, his father having been a professor of theology in Auburn Theological Seminary of the Presbyterian Church U.S.A., and his whole family was deeply rooted in the church. He was himself for some years the chairman of the National Council of Churches Commission on a Just and Durable Peace. In a time of world crisis he became Secretary of State under President Eisenhower with an opportunity to point world development in a Christian direction. But two competing loyalties were at war in him. With one side of his mind, the Christian side, he was passionately devoted to world peace, but with the other side, the national side, he was so imprisoned by a loyalty to the national interest that he found it impossible to approach even America's allies with anything except suspicion. He seemed devoid of the imagination that would enable him to look at an Egyptian situation through Egyptian eyes, a Chinese situation through Chinese eyes, or even a British situation through British eyes. He would not even speak to Chou En-lai of China at the Geneva Conference of 1954. With his blundering he kept the world teetering on the edge of an abyss for years.

But what interests us is that we should see reflected in that one man *our* failure as a church to develop a world outlook and a world concern in our members *as citizens,* consonant with the world outlook in evangelism and benevolence that we now take for granted. How much do we do to kindle in our people an interest in what is happening in the world beyond their borders and to develop in them the imagination that is able to enter into the situations of other peoples and to understand their attitudes, actions, and needs from the inside? Perhaps we do not think that is sufficiently religious in character to have a place in the educational and preaching program of the church. It seems too secular. We might call to mind that the action of the Samaritan in Jesus' famous parable was just such a secular action and that Jesus contrasted it with the engrossing religious concern of the priest and the Levite.

LOVE OF NEIGHBOR

In a public poll on the qualities of a good citizen, patriotism would be likely to place first but neighborliness would be a close second. And few would be likely to see the possibility of conflict between the two. In the Scriptures, love of neighbor is second only to love of God, is inseparable from love of God, and means, as we have just seen, a sharing with God of his care for his whole earthly family. But today love of neighbor is frequently separated from love of God and stands alone. Brotherhood has a sanctity only comparable with motherhood. No one in this land would ever dare speak a word against it.

Thus, Bonhoeffer's description of Jesus as "the man for others" has had an immense popularity. Even some Christian theologians speak as though love of neighbor were the essence of the New Testament gospel, forgetting entirely that, long before Jesus gave it classical expression in the parable of the good Samaritan, it was for centuries a primary element in the faith of Israel. Not only Jesus but also the rabbis held the two major commandments to be "Love God" and "Love your neighbor." Today the Biblical God has faded into the background and the proponents of a secularized Christianity make love of neighbor in the widest sense their central principle. If they let God stay in the picture at all, they usually identify him with the love that comes into being between the two neighbors. They have no doubts about man's capacity to love his neighbor.

Here it is essential to see the difference between a love of neighbor rooted and grounded in the love of God and a love of neighbor that is a general human potential. Humanitarianism has a history. Two centuries ago Rousseau and others were sponsors of a love of neighbor that would be quite independent of any Christian faith. It was regarded as an innate capacity of human beings that needed only to be encouraged. In the '20s of this century Irving Babbitt of Harvard in a number of his books, but especially in his *Democracy and Leadership,* found in this concept one of the most prolific sources of confusion in the modern world. He had no concern for Christian faith, only for what lets man be really human. He questioned the ability of any person to love his neighbor unless some powerful restraint were laid on the egotistical drives that are native to us all. To him such humanitarianism was a shallow sentimentalism, dangerous because of its lack of depth, so superficial that at the slightest resistance from the neighbor it was likely to be transformed into antagonism and hatred.

There is no expectation anywhere in Scripture that man by nature will love either his neighbor or his God. Adam, disobedient to his God in his bid for self-fulfillment, lays the blame on the only neighbor that he has. Cain inhumanly murders his own brother, and, when God asks him where Abel is, he answers, with the blood still on his hands, "I do not know; am I my brother's keeper?" Those are samples of the Bible's realism about man. Everywhere there is a positing that at the core of every human existence is a self that seeks its own sovereignty boldly and blindly, a self that must be overcome if man is to be really human. In New Testament terms, the self must die and be reborn if there is to be either love of God or love of neighbor.

It is here in the estimate of the natural potential of human nature that the Greek and the Hebrew mind part company. The Greek is an idealist, the Hebrew and Christian a realist. The Greek optimistically posits a divinity in man, at the very least a divine spark. The Hebrew more soberly reminds man of his creatureliness and of the gulf that his self-will sets between him and his God. Hidden in every man, no matter how devout, is not just a distance from God but a rebellion against God. Jesus discerns a Satan in his beloved Peter at the very moment when Peter is professing his willingness to die for him. Even a Nietzsche with his vision of a pagan superman could not quite forget the Christian insight that man is a being who must be conquered if he is to find himself. We are not by nature what we were meant to be in our creation. And that is why in both Testaments the love of God and the love of neighbor are inseparable and interdependent. We are so made that we cannot rightly have our neighbor without God, nor can we rightly have our God without our neighbor.

What must be grasped here is the interrelationship of the two levels on which we have our life. We live in our relationships. The deepest level of our life, whether we know it or not, is in our dialogue with God which underlies our whole existence. We do not even have to know his name to be responding to or rebelling against his bidding. The more immediate conscious level is in our dialogue with persons who constitute our world, though here again there are depths beyond our seeing. One thinks of the influence of intercessory prayer, a friendly hand reaching us unseen. Our dependence on human relations is obvious, though foolishly denied by some persons in their pride. Cut off from our relationships we begin to shrivel and die. A baby divorced from its mother, or from a substitute mother, is injured both psychically and physically. Adults placed in complete isolation begin gradually to disintegrate within themselves. Far more than we realize, our life is what it is because of what comes to us from others and what goes from us to others. But if this horizontal relation with other persons is essential to our existence from the first moments of our life, even more essential is the vertical relation with our God. Who can do for us what only he can do? Who else of all we know can meet us in that deep mysterious awesome center of our being where the ultimate decisions of our life are somehow made?

The simple truth is that the rightful center of our life is not in ourselves and cannot be in ourselves without distortion, perversion, and impoverishment of our life. It is beyond ourselves in God, the God whom we cannot have without our neighbor. We are so made that we cannot be truly ourselves, truly human, unless the doors are open on that deepest level and God's own nature is reflected in us, but when the doors are open there, they are open also on the level of the neighbor. Only in an unconditional openness to God is our natural self-centeredness sufficiently shattered that we become capable of loving our neighbor in spite of all that might make us hate him or ignore him. But equally true is it that unless we are willing to be there for our neighbor, really open to him, God is not willing to be there for us or open to us. It is this profound inner compulsion and liberation toward a neighborliness that knows no limits that is the most powerful shaping force in Christian citizenship.

THE CARE OF GOD'S WORLD

Another dimension of citizenship that takes us back into the Creation story is the relationship of man to nature. Man and woman, created to reflect God's own nature and to live in personal relation with him, are given the responsibility of maintaining order in the whole creation. In Psalm 8 the crowning glory of man's life is that he has been set over the works of God's hands. That element in the Creation story has in recent years been held responsible for the development of very bad citizenship in Christians in their relation to nature. Prof. Lynn T. White has indicted it as the source of modern man's ruthless exploitation of nature, dominion over the earth being taken by Christians to be a divine permission to plunder the resources of the planet. Also, former Associate Justice W. O. Douglas, a zealous guardian of the natural environment, especially in the mountain regions dear to him from his childhood on, has lashed out in his autobiography against the Christian religion as being in its very constitution careless of nature. The charge arises from a faulty reading of Gen. 1:28. That verse in which mankind is given dominion has to be understood in the context of the whole Creation story. Man and woman as God's representatives are charged to maintain order in God's world and to care for it on his behalf. They are not independent entrepreneurs free to do with it whatever they like. They are stewards responsible to God for the discharge of their commission. Accountability is of the very essence of their relationship with God. But it must trouble us that a professor and a justice of the Supreme Court, both incidentally sons of Presbyterian ministers, should so misunderstand the Creation story. How was it possible for them to be so misinformed?

An experience of my own throws light on the problem. Several years ago Prof. James Barr gave a lecture in Union Theological Seminary, New York, dealing specifically with

Professor White's accusation. By a scholarly examination of the language of Gen., ch. 1, he demonstrated the untenability of White's thesis. Following the lecture a group of professors and students were discussing what they had heard when I noticed under the arm of a student a paperback commentary on Genesis that I had not seen before. I took it from him and opened it at Gen. 1:28. To our amazement, there in the commentary Gen. 1:28 was interpreted as giving to mankind the right to *exploit* the resources of the earth. The very word "exploit" was used. Rather soberly we asked ourselves how many interpreters in the past had extracted that meaning from the text. Greed, or even just economic aggressiveness, does not need any more explicit religious validation than that to justify an unlimited rape of nature for the sake of personal or corporate profit.

The misinterpretation is a warning to us of how subtly the economic context can twist the meaning of Scripture in the mind of the preacher so that the church is found condoning a false development when it should be exposing and criticizing it. Professor White and Justice Douglas should have laid their charges, not against the Scriptures and Christianity, but against a false teaching or a silence of the church. A Biblically grounded Christianity is not careless of the natural environment but should be its guardian. The animals, the fish, the birds, the trees, the flowers, the fruits of the land are God's before they are ours. And because they are God's creatures, they are to be ever approached with respect and thankfulness. The care of God's world must stand high among the responsibilities of the Christian citizen.

A MAN SENT

Earlier we saw a succession of crosses scattered throughout the Scriptures, giving to them a significant unity. Behind each of those crosses is a story of courageous public service that began with a call from God. The history is set in motion by these calls. Moses confronts God on the mountainside in Sinai and hears the call to lead his people out of slavery in Egypt. Samuel is called to guide the transition of his nation from a loose federation of tribes into a unified monarchy. Prophets, priests, and kings are called to their several tasks. John the Baptist, born a priest, is called to be a prophet. Jesus, a carpenter, in his baptismal experience is called to his mission and, like others before him, is endowed with power to fulfill it in the experience of being called. Disciples are called to share in Jesus' mission. Paul is called to be the apostle of Jesus to the Gentiles. But comprehending all these calls and reaching out to include countless men and women through the centuries is the call of Israel as a people in covenant with God which Christians see in continuity with the call of the church to be the special instrumentality of God's saving purpose in the midst of the world. The man of the Scriptures, whether he be Jew or Christian, is a man with a special vocation. He has a special responsibility as a citizen. If he has come to personal knowledge of this Biblical God, then he knows himself called and sent to fulfill in some way God's purpose for his world.

The chosenness of Israel as God's people has to be understood in the light of the individual calls. This has frequently been forgotten in uses that have been made of the concept of a chosen people. We understand God's choice of Israel and the unique sending of the church only when we have let it be interpreted by the choice and sending of a Moses, a Jeremiah, a Jesus, and a Paul. Israel was a chosen people only insofar as it shared this prophetic and priestly calling and cherished within it the tradition of being witnesses to God's awesome yet gracious purpose for the whole world. The church inherited this same destiny only insofar as it surrendered itself in each new age to be a fresh embodiment of the mission of Jesus. God's need is for a people bound to him unconditionally, responsive to his bidding, enlightened by his truth, hating every form of inhumanity as he hates it and loving people as he loves them. This chosen people is the

primary channel of his action in history. He can and does act
through other channels, but here he has a people consciously
responsible to be the channel of his action. He has called
them. He has chosen them. He has bound them to him so that
they can never be free from him again, yet in a binding that
to them is their liberation to be most truly themselves.
Through them he purposes to get his work done in the world.
This lies at the heart of any doctrine of the church.

But this concept of a chosen people has been sadly per-
verted in both ancient and modern times. In ancient Israel
it was debased by the popular religious imagination to a level
indistinguishable from any other nation's belief concerning
itself, that God and nation were bound together in a common
destiny in which the god could no more get free from the
nation than the nation could get free from the god. The
greatness of Israel's God thus enhanced the self-esteem of
Israelites and gave them confidence in a glorious future.
Early in this century many theologians and even some Old
Testament scholars saw nothing more than that in Israel's
conviction of chosenness, a primitive form of national egotism. But one of the achievements of Biblical theology has
been to recognize the decisive importance of the doctrine of
election in the unfolding not only of Israel's history but also
the very existence of the church.

The modern perversion of the concept may be more familiar to us, though we may not realize how deeply rooted it is
in our Protestant religious history. During the past three
hundred years there has been a widespread assumption in
our English-speaking world that white Anglo-Saxon Protestants are a modern version of the chosen people of God,
called by him to manage the world on his behalf. There has
been both a British and an American version of this and both
have had far-reaching consequences both politically and
economically. In each the chosenness has been transferred
from church to nation, the basis for the transfer being a
confidence that the nation had already been essentially
Christianized.

One of my personal perplexities is how for years I could have been a minister, a Biblical scholar, and a Christian theologian and have remained unaware of how influential this assumption was in the life of our Protestant community. The only form in which it made itself directly visible was in a certain ridiculous "crackpot" organization called the "British Israelites" which claimed that the English nation was directly descended from the lost ten tribes of Israel, its language a development from Hebrew, and that the British monarch, being directly in line with King David, was divinely ordained to rule eventually over the whole earth. Not until I read Robert T. Handy's *A Christian America* and Martin Marty's *Righteous Empire* did I begin to awaken to how and why a more subtle and respectable form of this national egotism is embedded in the very substructure of our English-speaking Protestant existence.

We have already seen how this development began three centuries ago or more, when church and state were closely identified and it was taken for granted that a nation with an established church of which all its citizens were members was automatically a Christian nation. With this background and with Puritan Bible-reading citizens seeing their national experiences mirrored in the Old Testament history of Israel, it was almost inevitable that they would begin to think of themselves as a modern Israel. Both in Britain and in America this identification with Israel and this confidence in being now God's chosen people, heightened by a general assurance that the purest version of Christianity was preserved in the British tradition, issued (in widely separated eras) in the assumption that *(a)* Britain and *(b)* the United States were charged with the responsibility of preserving order in God's world and sharing with all lesser privileged nations the benefits of a Christian faith and a Christian civilization. While the Christian faith was communicated by an evangelism that converted the natives, the Christian civilization required the incorporation of these peoples into a new political and economic order. Thus, in both Britain and America this consciousness of national destiny produced on the one hand a missionary enterprise of the churches to evangelize the world but, on the other hand and in close coordination, an imperial outreach which dreamed of the whole world eventually sharing a common life with God's new Israel. It was an intoxicating dream. The Biblical vision of a new Eden on earth would be realized in a truly democratic society where all were free, and, once realized, would be shared generously with the rest of mankind. The remarkable prosperity of Britain in the nineteenth century and of America in the twentieth and the advance in both of increasingly liberal and beneficent forms of democracy encouraged the conviction that God was indeed showing a special favor toward his chosen representatives and blessing them in a singularly obvious fashion. Victory in two successive wars reinforced this conviction in the popular mind.

A more careful reading of the Old Testament—and the New—would have prevented this misdirection of Christian citizenship and this dangerous encouragement of national egos. It might well have been noticed that Israel *as a nation* was consistently unwilling to fulfill the destiny for which it was chosen, national interests always getting in the way. Only a minority within Israel, a remnant, maintained through the centuries the continuity of the divine destiny. Always, as is evident in the picture of the Servant Israel in Isa., ch. 53, it was at heavy cost in humiliation and suffering. But as long as the illusion persisted that our nations were Christian nations and our civilization a Christian civilization, we remained prisoners of this false conception of our destiny and our status. Not until the '20s of this century did we begin to get free of these illusions, and even yet they exercise a power in the national life that has serious international consequences. The Jewish people today and in particular the Israelis might look with care at these Christian misinterpretations of what it means to be the chosen people of God. The transfer of the concept from the prophetic remnant to the nation as a "whole," ours or theirs, is a misreading of the divine intention that leads inevitably to disastrous exploits and adventures.

THE SOURCE OF OUR FREEDOM

The divine calling, however, which makes both Jews and Christians a covenant people of God is the very foundation of their freedom. It is important that it is in a word which he speaks to us that God binds us to him in this covenant relation. He sets his mark upon us. He makes his truth a fiery presence within us from which we can never again get free. He kindles within us his own passion for justice. He makes us his people through whom he intends to get his work done in the world. Entering into a relationship such as that with God might seem to mean the end of our freedom. But because the relationship is sustained by a word and words, that is, as a personal relationship, and the compulsion we experience is that of an infinite truth and justice and mercy which are the very essence of what it means to be human, our submission to God is our liberation to be most completely ourselves as human beings. By binding us to himself God makes us free with a freedom that is indestructible. That is the paradox of Christian freedom. Jeremiah, once enlightened by God with the truth essential to be heard in the Judean situation, was not free to be silent. God's word was like a fire in his bones that could not be kept in. Paul became the slave of Jesus Christ and from that moment found himself the freest of all men in his new humanity. Jesus, the prophets, and the apostles are a succession of princes of freedom, and through them the Scriptures become a school of freedom in every age.

There are two kinds of freedom that are often confused and need to be sharply distinguished. There are people who choose to be free and there are people who because of a prior choice by God have no alternative but to be free. The former see freedoms of various kinds as essential to the kind of democratic world in which they wish to have their life. A regimented world is obnoxious to them. They choose freedom. But it is *their* choice and there could be circumstances in which they might find it advisable, at least for a time, to surrender their freedoms in some measure. They do not have to be free. But the succession of persons who meet us in the Scriptures have no choice but to be free. Like Martin Luther they have to say, "So help me God, I can do no other." For Jesus the price of freedom to fulfill his destiny was the crucifixion. There are freedoms that are guaranteed to us by the laws of our land and we must guard them jealously, but they would not exist had there not been persons who had to speak and act in freedom when the laws and the authorities in their communities condemned their words and actions. The preservation of freedom for the future is likely to depend not so much upon citizens who choose to be free as upon men and women with this inner binding that compels them to be free.

There is a superficial kind of freedom that is frequently confused with Christian freedom but actually is almost its opposite. In its extreme form it claims for the individual a freedom from all binding, human or divine. Every man a king! A former President wrote a book on liberty fifty years ago in which he defined liberty as the God-given right of every person to do what he wills with his own life and with everything that is his own, without let or hindrance from any quarter. That appealed strongly to an individualistic society. Actually it is the Magna Charta of anarchy, a rugged individualism which dissolves all social restraints. Most of the advances in the last fifty years in the humanization of our society have set restrictions on that kind of freedom, but it is still widely claimed in many areas of life. Economically we must be prepared for even greater restrictions if even a beginning is to be made in redressing the imbalance between the haves and the have-nots in our world. Churches that minister largely to the haves and whose members are rarely in contact with the have-nots are likely still to leave unchallenged the old individualistic brand of freedom and to produce few citizens who understand or propagate the humbler and more responsible freedom that should stem directly from their faith.

TRADITION AND FREEDOM

The truth about all of us, however, is that we are never as free as we think we are. Our whole existence, Christian or non-Christian, is webbed into a network of traditions that determine, far more than we ever realize, how we think and feel and act. We are born into a complex of traditions—family traditions, community traditions, racial traditions, national traditions, church traditions—and our whole being is shaped by them long before we are conscious of what is happening. We Protestants often assume that only Catholics and Jews have a problem with tradition. For us the word of God in Scripture is our only guide! But in so thinking, we blind ourselves to our own imprisonment in traditions and remain unaware of the extent to which they are determining our decisions. In many instances even our interpretation of Scripture represents an unexamined and untested conformity with a tradition that we have inherited from the past.

There is no escape for any of us from tradition in any department of our life. Every home has a tradition. It is the product of two earlier traditions, plus other influences. It begins to take shape in the first moments of a marriage and once formed is not easy to change. It gives to each family its distinctive character. And every Christian congregation has a tradition. What drives ministers to despair, and many members too, is the tenacity of traditions inherited from the past that have neither Christian nor rational justification and are boulders in the way of future development. So also, every profession has a tradition, and every institution, every community, every nation. In no area of life do we have the opportunity of starting from scratch. And we do not even know who we are until we have explored the traditions that have shaped us and our world. That is why history is of such great importance to us. It does not grip us until we read it as the story of our own coming into being.

But all tradition, because it is human tradition, has a contradictory character. It has within it both the promise of our future and the negation of any future for us other than a continuation of the existing order of our life. Persons imbued with the spirit of reform are likely to think of tradition mainly in negative terms, as the dead hand of the past, as that which freezes all the structures of life. We need Tevye of *Fiddler on the Roof* to dramatize for us its positive, constructive significance. "Tradition, tradition, that's what makes us what we are," he sings. Tradition for him and for all his people is the treasure-house of the wisdom and experience of the past. It is the source of their stability and of their capacity for survival under inhuman pressures. But tradition for Tevye and for us can also be a prison house forcing us to go on living with the mistakes, prejudices, and stupidities of the past.

The Scriptures are a school of freedom because of the way in which they constantly combine an openness to the past with an equal openness to the future, a profound respect for tradition with a willingness to rebel against tradition. History and eschatology are both essential for the prophetic insight that keeps Israel ever moving forward toward its distant goal. Faith looks back to see the line of destiny marked out by God, but also to see where the destiny has been betrayed, that there may be a surer and more faithful journey into the future.

Nothing is more impressive than the way in which this servant people of God kept steadily moving on, in spite of monstrous obstacles, failures, and disasters, with a singleness of purpose. Why is it that never for long are they prisoners of their past but ever break out afresh to begin another stage in their long journey? Gerhard von Rad, in his history of the Israelite traditions, has portrayed for us this restless movement, each stage in the formation and expression of Israel's faith being forced to surrender to a new development, each in turn preserving the insights of the past yet breaking decisively with elements that had to be left behind. There is no mystery about what made this possible. It is the relativizing of all history by the Israelite faith in a transcendent God, a God whose purpose for his people transcends every possible religious and secular establishment. There was always a prophet to proclaim the distance between God's thoughts and man's thoughts and therefore between the divine intention and the human construction. The dynamic of Israel's history lay in the tension between God and man.

The events portrayed in the New Testament constitute a final breakthrough and reformulation of the Israelite tradition. The closest Israel ever came to absolutizing the order of its life was in the first centuries B.C. and A.D., when on the basis of an infallible Scripture (the idea of infallibility having been imported from Greece), there came to be an infallible tradition that enclosed life in a network of infallible laws. It was in perfect keeping with the character of the earlier history that that should be the moment when, after six centuries of silence, the Israelite prophetic order should find its voice again in John the Baptist and the prophetic word should become incarnate in Jesus, disrupting the absolutes that had frozen the pattern of life and had brought the journey of God's people to a halt. The Christian gospel and the Christian church as they come to expression in the New Testament must be understood as a massive reinterpretation and reformulation of the Israelite tradition.

That sets the pattern not only for the Christian church as it continues on its way toward its goal but for all our dealings with tradition. If we believe in the Biblical God and have learned to see all things in our life in the light of his nature and his intention, there can never for us be any absolutizing of the existing order. In the church and far beyond the church we are constantly made uncomfortable by the contradictions between divine intention and our human performance and construction. The consequences of this for our citizenship are obvious. A Christian citizen cannot be a thoughtless supporter of the *status quo*. His faith in God generates in him a critical mind that sifts the traditions of the past and tests them by criteria that are the product of his Biblical faith.

Theologians today for whom all talk of God is purposeless, meaningless, and inane, or who tell us that a faith relevant to a twentieth-century world must get rid of the transcendent God, cannot have studied with any care either the history of Israel or the history of the Christian church. It is the transcendent God, the God who is other than man, who is over against man, who brings man under judgment before he discloses to him his mercy, who is the living God with power to set man free from the imprisoning and impoverishing structures of his life.

It may be interesting and impressive to hear testimony to this from an atheist. One of the participants in the dialogues of recent years between Communist philosophers and Christian theologians in Eastern Europe has been the Czechoslovakian atheist philosopher Milan Machovec. Speaking in New York some years ago, he complained that, in the dialogues, too often the Christian theologians soft-pedaled the subject of God. They thought they must find elsewhere the point of contact and the area of discussion where they might reach some measure of mutual understanding. "But," said Machovec, "it is your faith in a transcendent God that interests us more than anything else, because we recognize in it the dynamic of your society. It is the relativization of all your present achievements by this element of the transcendent that frees you to make fresh ventures into the future. That is what our Communist society lacks. It is essential for our future that we find a secular equivalent for your transcendent God."

Here then is perhaps the most important contribution of these Scriptures to a citizenship that soon will stand at the beginning of a new century. How can this new century be really new? How can citizens find freedom within themselves for the reshaping of a world that has upon it so many of the signs of death? If they would have the humility to learn from this Israel of God in Scripture, they would discover that only when we let all the traditions of the past come under the searching judgment of God do we begin to hear the promise of the future that he has yet in store for us. And for us as nations that judgment meets us most effectively in the cross of Jesus Christ, the climactic moment of revelation in Israel.

4

The Present Dilemma

CIVIL RELIGION ONCE MORE

The more clearly we spell out the nature of a Biblically based Christian citizenship, the more sharply does the difference become apparent between it and a citizenship based on even the most idealistic form of civil religion. Early or late, civil religion inevitably takes on a nationalistic character. Robert Bellah may dream of it being so high-minded that it would one day break out beyond the borders of America and become an acceptable religion for many nations. But by its very nature such religion is the spiritual substructure and justification of one society, deeply rooted in its history and unlikely to capture the devotion of anyone who does not in some measure share that history. It is a state religion and, however superior the ideals and values that are incorporated in it, it has to take its place in the succession of state religions that stretches all the way from Egypt and Rome down to our own day. More than once in the past, beginning with Constantine in the fourth century, the Christian church has been conscripted to become a state religion, gracing the state with its transcendent authority and justifying the order of its life as divinely ordained, but always there has been an ineradicable memory in the church of what it was intended to be when its Lord, on his way to be crucified by the officials of the state, gave himself to it to be forevermore the restless leaven of its existence. The Lord who in his risen power hides himself in the body of his church eventually resists and thwarts every attempt of the world to take his church captive and to use it for its own purposes. We owe a debt to Robert Bellah, therefore, for having brought out so clearly into the open what until now has been shrouded and foggy, that there is in America a civil or state religion, with its own history and character, its own scriptures, priests, and ritual, to be distinctly differentiated from either Christianity or Judaism.

It must be clear, however, that the rejection of any such state religion—and it is more conducive to clear thinking if we call it "state religion" rather than "civil religion"—is not by any means a rejection of the values and principles that have been incorporated in it. Examine carefully the ingredients of what Bellah calls "civil religion" and you become quickly aware that they are the ethical products of three great religious and philosophical traditions—Christianity, Judaism, and humanism. To steal Elton Trueblood's term, this state religion is not an independent growth but is a "cut-flower religion." The flowers that have been grown in the Christian church, the Jewish synagogue, and the groves of the great humanist philosophers are cropped and used to grace the temple of the state religion—the passion for justice, the dignity of the human person, the hatred of tyranny, the demand for freedom, the love of the neighbor, the tolerance of differences, the pursuit of world peace, compassion for the needy. These are not the products of any state religion of the last two hundred years but are rooted in faiths that go back three thousand years and more. Divorced from their native origins, detached from their theological roots, they are likely only to wither and die. It is one of the illusions of our secular society and also of some secular theology of today that we have reached a state of spiritual and intellectual maturity where we can enjoy all the ethical fruits of Christianity and Judaism without having to bother ourselves with the complications of a relationship with the living God of either the prophets or the apostles.

We must say a word also about the problem that civil religion is purported to solve. We are told that it is the necessary glue to hold together the divergent elements in a pluralistic society. Its proponents are seized with a fear that society is dissolving into fragments. But it requires no more than a moment's consideration to recognize that this state religion, far from being a bond of unity, must inevitably be a bone of contention as soon as it stands forth as what it is. It has its strength only when it is able to masquerade as Christian or Jewish or humanist. But as soon as it declares its independence of Christianity, Judaism, and humanism, as Bellah says it must, and claims to be a state or civil religion for all, it becomes openly a religious rival of all three, competing for the loyalty of all citizens.

The humanist is not likely to have much respect for a God who is so transparently merely a supernatural prop for the ideals and values that are considered essential to the national life. The Christian who knows why he is a Christian will know that he cannot divide his allegiance between Christ and a state religion. And the Jew, who so recently has suffered severely at the hands of a barbarous state religion, will see only too clearly the direction in which such a development is likely to go. The Christian, the Jew, and the humanist can find their way to a unity of purpose as citizens of their nation much more effectively when with a full recognition of their religious diversity they take account of all that they share and treasure in their common heritage.

Civil religion has no place in it for a cross. But for a Biblical faith and a Biblically based citizenship the cross of Jesus Christ and the crosses of prophets and apostles constantly give warning of how easily a devotion to the national interest can blind a nation to its true destiny. The cross is the place where Christians discover what it is in themselves and in their neighbors that can rob them, as individuals, as a community, as a nation, of their future. Where civil religion with its idealism reassures the civil religionist of his virtue as an idealist, the crucified Lord, if he has his way with the Christian citizen, humbles him utterly, robs him of all confidence in his own virtue, and lays him open so unconditionally to God and to the coming of God's Kingdom on earth that his first loyalty as a citizen is to the dawning of that new age. Moreover, the cross warns him of powers, influences, and loyalties hidden beneath the surface of every nation's life that have in them the potentiality of erecting new crosses in the modern world. Therefore, the Christian makes his most valuable and distinctive contribution to the life of his community, not by setting aside the elements that are unique in his Christianity so that in his citizenship he may be united with all his fellow citizens in a common faith, but rather by bringing to the common life the profoundest insights that have been generated by his faith.

One of the claims constantly made for civil religion is that, being devoid of sectarian characteristics, it can and should be taught in all the schools of America. It is safe to say that, without any such encouragement, it is already taught in many of the schools of America. But this makes a mockery of the Constitution, which forbids the teaching of any one religion in the schools. Both church and synagogue should take with seriousness that, insofar as civil religion is, as Bellah insists, a religion distinctly other than Christianity or Judaism, it is a rival of Christianity and Judaism encouraging the worship of a God who cannot be identified with the God of Israel or the God and Father of Jesus Christ. Therefore, to promote an alliance today between the Christian church and a deistic public piety, as Richard John Neuhaus and others do, is to continue in a new form the confusion of church and nation that has persisted in the past and to leave Christians divided in their loyalty between the god of public piety, who provides the necessary supernatural support for the American experiment, and the God of the prophets, the God and Father of Jesus, who at one and the same time sets the American experiment radically in question and is the one and only hope of its ultimate fulfillment. What must be realized is that public piety based on civil religion does not issue in the same kind of citizenship as does faith in Jesus Christ, crucified and risen. But neither does that distinctive faith separate Christians from their fellow citizens whose lives are nourished from other sources; rather, it sends Christians into the community ready to cooperate with all who in any degree share the vision of a world in which every form of injustice and inhumanity will be resisted and overcome.

THE LARGER PERIL

Being worried and fearful about national unity, about the disillusionment of youth with patriotism and about the despair of the intelligentsia with their nation's future, when the whole world is facing monstrous and perilous problems, is like distressing oneself about the weeds in one's private garden when the whole city round about is on fire. The human race is in real trouble and there is no form of protection—military, political, economic, social, or religious—that can exempt any nation from involvement in it. We have been so busy building our glamorous modern world we did not notice that with its increasing complexity came a corresponding fragility. A few years ago the lights went out in whole regions of Central Canada and Eastern United States. The elevators in New York skyscrapers stopped working. Some Canadian spokesmen chose that moment to denounce our dependence upon our neighbor. To their chagrin, it turned out to be a breakdown in Niagara Falls, Canada, that had put out all the lights and stopped all the elevators on the Eastern seaboard. The incident was prophetic of what can happen in a world where the lines of interdependence have become so many. For years we have been building our cities and our industries so that they run on oil and, in them, all movement comes to a halt if there is no oil. We built as though the supply of oil were inexhaustible—and as though forever the producers of the oil would be reasonable about its price. Therefore, it was like an awakening from a deep sleep when suddenly, angered by the Western world's support of Israel, the Arab oil-producing countries radically increased the price of oil and threatened to place an embargo on its export. The economies of all the Western nations were unbalanced. Some, such as Britain and Italy, were threatened with bankruptcy. And industrial development in many Third World countries was brought to a halt. We had not expected the Arabs to be so unmannerly. In response there was even a hysteria at high levels that led to talk of a military takeover of some of the oil fields!

The same fragility has been accentuated by atomic bombs and atomic energy production. The atomic bomb, which in time became the much more destructive hydrogen bomb, was to have made us safe from external attack, and atomic energy was to have provided a limitless supply of power to fuel the engines of our world. But now the bomb and its horrendous children are suspended over us and all our neighbors like a million million Swords of Damocles, and the cost of maintaining the defense systems of an atomic age threatens to exhaust the treasuries of nations large and small. Also, while atomic power stations proliferate, no scientist as yet has found a feasible way of disposing of the atomic wastes which will not lose their deadly and destructive character for one hundred thousand years! An exiled Russian scientist in London, England, has recently revealed that in 1958, somewhere in Siberia, a deposit of these wastes overheated and exploded with disastrous consequences.

Then there is the current combination of inflation and depression before which even the most expert experts seem to be helpless. John Maynard Keynes with his invention of deficit financing was supposed to have put an end to such economic derangements. Solve the problems of the present by borrowing from the future! Our posterity, who will have to pay the bills eventually, has no way of refusing to lend to us! But the future has a way of becoming the present and, when it does, it has its own costly programs. As if that were not enough, there comes the warning that there are limits to the growth of the gross national product, whose expansion is so essential to the maintenance of prosperity—also that the higher it goes in our lands, the wider becomes the gap between our island of prosperity and the ocean of poverty that surrounds us and increasingly threatens us. How long will those billions of human beings in the Third World be content to watch us eat and waste while they remain half starved? Their numbers increase much more rapidly than ours. By the year 2000 the population of the Third World will have doubled—four billion hungry men, women, and children instead of two billion! And in the face of such international problems, we worry about our national unity! It would be more appropriate, and more Christian, for us to worry about our national vision, our national sanity, and our ability to see and to act effectively in such a world as this.

Aleksandr Solzhenitsyn, with his savage exposures of the inhuman practices of Soviet Russia, for a time delighted and horrified the Western world and, unintentionally, ministered to its complacency. But more recently he has turned his critique upon us and has predicted catastrophe for us unless we open our eyes and face our problems with a very different spirit. Robert L. Heilbroner, of the New School for Social Research in New York, has in several publications made a masterly review of the world situation and from present information has projected the character of the challenges—social, economic, political, ecological—that will have to be faced in the next twenty-five, fifty, or one hundred years. Their dimensions are to him so terrifying that he despairs of any form of democratic organization being adequate to carry through the social and economic reorganization that will be necessary if they are to be mastered. But his despair is rather premature. It does not seem to occur to him that the record of authoritarian governments in this century in meeting and solving the problems of human society does not encourage an expectation of help from that quarter.

We need these warnings to waken us to our human predicament because our wealth and our power have made us singularly insensitive, blind, and overconfident. Our Christian faith has contributed also to this overconfidence insofar as it has led us to think of our part of the world as already Christian, blessed with its riches because it is Christian, and protected forever against all perils by its own Christian God! But if we know anything of the resources that are hidden in the Christian faith, we should know that it is a faith for just such a time as this. The Christian whose life is nourished by the Scriptures shares the faith of Israel's prophets, psalmists, historians, and wise men and of Christian apostles and evangelists. Therefore he, his community, his nation, and his age stand ever under the judgment of God, which lays bare, far more profoundly than any social scientist can, the corruptions that endanger their life and in fact make impossible any healthful future. But God's judgment, in distinction from the most careful sociological assessment, is an expression also of his mercy and issues not in despair but in hope of new beginnings beyond the hour of judgment. Therefore the Christian, while he may see the present moment as a time of fearful judgment upon the blindness and errors of the past, is not driven to despair or to such desperate remedies as totalitarian rule, but only to a humbling repentance that makes him open to a rethinking of his approach to all the problems of his world.

Also, the Christian is unconquerable in the hour of crisis because he places his confidence for the future not in the durability of his civilization or the strength of his nation but in the God whose purpose steadily unfolds in history while nations and civilizations are born, flourish, and pass away. There have been Christians, even Christian theologians, who have despaired of any future for Christianity should Western civilization crumble and perish. To them the threat of godless Communism has been the threat of annihilation for any Christian future. But that is to see the primary threat to our future beyond ourselves when it is always in ourselves, in the character of our Christian faith, in the mores of our society, and in the contradictions and blindnesses of our civilization.

Part of our problem has been the confidence, engendered in us by the triumphs of our science and technology, in the power of intelligence to meet and master all problems. But the problems that are most crucial for the future of mankind are not of such a character that they can be solved by intelligence alone. There is the problem of colossal military expenditures, more than one hundred billions per year in the United States and thirty billions in Russia, while Russians are deprived of adequate food and housing and American cities are threatened with bankruptcy. In ten years or less, inflation alone will push that American figure to two hundred billion. Why this insane escalation? There is no other answer than fear, a fear that is escalated on both sides as each seeks to forge ahead of the other and be safe against attack. There is no longer any way to be safe against attack. Then, to keep the armament factories running at full speed, Russia and the United States have become the chief salesmen of arms and planes to the smaller nations, which can ill afford the wastage of their resources. In one year the United States sold ten billion dollars' worth of arms to countries in the region of the Persian Gulf. The transaction helped to pay for oil, but what it did for human beings in that part of the world is another matter.

Intelligence has not been conspicuous in the management of our cities. Again the Keynesian theory of "Enjoy now, pay later" has generated a euphoria in which no one seems to have calculated that future generations would have their own bills to pay. How could a city such as New York, with all its wealth and with all its intelligent citizens, let its affairs get into such a hopeless tangle that only state and national rescue operations can save it from bankruptcy? Why was there no word of warning years ago? And why no word of warning about the polluting of our rivers, lakes, and oceans, as well as our air? The pollution goes forward at a rate that, unchecked, could finally make the entire globe uninhabitable. We have been the victims of the illusion that the resources of our world are unlimited. The astronauts in their tiny ship with its severely limited resources, looking back at the world slowly turning in space and seeing it as a somewhat larger spaceship but also limited severely and needing to exercise caution for the sake of its survival, should have shocked us awake to our situation. But talk of limited resources is not popular. Caution so easily is regarded as economic treason. Modern scientific man with his romantic conception of himself as master of his world can acknowledge no limits without abandoning the creed by which he lives.

It is surprising that the two world wars into which we stumbled in this century have not made Western man question more sharply the power of his intelligence and the wisdom of his principles. Those conflicts were not accidents. The history of the preceding years makes clear that they were the inevitable fruits of the kind of world we were. But why did we have to be that kind of world? It was not the so-called unchristian, uncivilized nations that spawned these wars; they did not have the will or the wealth or the weapons to fight such wars. Nations that until recently insisted they were Christian nations have been the ones that in this twentieth century have wasted in war the resources of the earth and destroyed the lives of tens of millions. The record of our citizenship in this century is not good. There has been and there still is something seriously wrong. Privately, in our homes and in our local communities we—Americans, Germans, Frenchmen, Britons, Canadians, Russians—have as a rule been good citizens, honest, hard-working, generous to the needy, anxious to preserve good order, reasonable in solving local problems where we ourselves are immediately concerned. But in the public sphere, where the decisions are made that govern the social, economic, and political future of all of us, the whole area is sprinkled with disasters. It is as though we had our eyes only half open, so that, entranced by the technological advances that seem to be creating a marvelous new world for us and convinced that our century is in every way the century of progress, we remain blind to the dimension of the evils and the perils that threaten our future.

THE INDICTMENT AGAINST US AS CHRISTIANS

Christians do not have to punish themselves for not yet having rid the world of all its evils. That the evils are still so great after nearly two thousand years of Christianity is sometimes cited as evidence of its failure. But that is to underestimate the depth and magnitude of the problem and to set a timetable for God. The Scriptures surely warn us how formidable and stubborn are the forces that must be overcome. After all, it took the covenant people of God more than a thousand years just to make their tortuous way from the deserts of Sinai where they had their birth to the church of Antioch where they finally burst forth into the world scene. And in the nineteen hundred years since then, who else has been working with an even similar earnestness at the problem? The gospel provides no blueprint for the reconstruction of the world. But what it does provide is a revelation in Jesus Christ, in his person and above all in his death and resurrection, of how a true humanity is to be realized, in openness to God and to the neighbor, and how the inhumanity that is the source of all our distress is to be overcome.

The revelation is not in Jesus Christ alone, but bonded together with him are witnesses to the same reality in the Old Testament, anticipating him, and in the New, remembering him and uniting with him. Therefore, what can and should be expected of Christians is that they should have their eyes open, that is, that they should actually have received and responded to the revelation and therefore should be acutely aware of the infinite and agonizing contradiction between humanity and inhumanity. Like Paul they should know that they struggle not against flesh and blood—that is, evil that can be recognized with the outward eye—but against principalities and powers, evil and destructive forces that can hide themselves under the cloak of legality, public welfare, patriotism, and religious earnestness.

The prophet Ezekiel gives us a likeness to describe the Christian's responsibility before God when he portrays himself as a watchman on the wall of the city. While others sleep he stands guard against danger both from without and from within. God charges him to sound the warning when danger appears and holds him responsible for the safety of the city. If he fails to warn the people of their danger, their deaths will be charged against him. That imagery can be transferred to the Christian church. Care for the world reflecting God's care for his world is the very heart of the gospel, and care for the world means surely a constant watchfulness over its life to recognize and resist the evils that threaten it, not when they have already set the world ablaze but when they are in their incipient stages. Even a fragmentary review of the twentieth century suggests that there has been a singular tardiness on the part of Christians in the discharge of this watchman function.

THE SLOWNESS OF CHRISTIANS TO OPEN THEIR EYES

I can speak from personal experience of how slow Christians were in the first half of this century, in Canada and in the United States, to open their eyes to the inhuman conditions being endured by unorganized labor. The problem reaches far back into the nineteenth century. In the latter half of that century England had had an awakening when Frederick Denison Maurice and Charles Kingsley with their Christian socialism and Charles Dickens with his novels exposed the miseries of the working poor. Kingsley in one of his reports described workmen in London in the 1860's with open sewers under their houses from which they drew the water for their household use! Before the century ended, a powerful social conscience had been called awake in the British churches and beyond them in the highest intellectual circles. But it was not until nearly the turn of the century that a similar awakening began in North America with a Walter

Rauschenbusch and a Washington Gladden as its apostles.

The resistance to it here was stronger than in Britain. As late as the 1930's, most churchmen were still reluctant to speak out even in defense of the workingman's right by organizing to obtain some guarantee of his economic security. The governing bodies of local churches were composed more often of executives than of workingmen and they made no secret of what they expected of their minister. They would tolerate general appeals for justice but not encouragement of any specific action to secure justice in the local situation. Few ministers can look back with comfort on their silence in those years. Symptomatic of the general situation was the experience of a labor organizer in the Pittsburgh region. In 1945 I heard from him his story of how when he and his family moved to Pittsburgh the members of the church they chose to attend did everything in their power to indicate to them that they were not welcome. Labor organizers were simply troublemakers, even when they claimed to be Christians. Good church people did not want the church associated with such disturbers. It did not occur to them that they were binding the church with the interests of the employers. But in this instance there was a happy outcome. The pastor was awake and let the confrontation bring debate and an exploration of the issues, which had far-reaching consequences for the congregation's social outlook.

The economic problem that now looms ever larger is the international one. Air travel, radio, television, and the proliferation of transnational corporations have shrunk the dimensions of our globe so that countries that were once far distant, out of sight and thought, are now our next-door neighbors. Many of them have had to borrow from us for their development and through our loans and outright gifts have fallen into a relation of dependence upon us that seriously constricts their freedom. Chile, for instance, having been encouraged to borrow nearly half a billion each year from the United States, was plunged into chaos when suddenly most of that support was withdrawn, and from the chaos emerged

a tyrannical military government. Most Third World countries are now deeply in debt to the governments and banks
of our wealthier Western nations and, when they cannot
repay the debts on time, they come directly under our economic and political control. Yet we are also dependent upon
them, for our prosperity is fueled by the resources we draw
from them and the goods and services we export to them.
The very use of the term "Third World" is misleading, suggesting as it does another world from ours, remote from us,
when in actuality it is now a constituent part of the world for
which we have the major share of responsibility. A situation
emerges internationally that is parallel to that which existed
within Britain, Germany, and America in the late nineteenth century. Just as Christians then were blind to the
growing gap between rich and poor in their own nations, so
now we who enjoy the affluence of our part of the world are
very slow to see the misery of hundreds of millions whose
economies are knit together with our own and whose poverty promotes our profits. In North America, with 6 percent
of the world's population, we have about 32 percent of the
world's wealth, and, in spite of all our acts of benevolence,
each year we become wealthier and the poor nations become
poorer.

Let us set alongside each other two scenes, one from Peru,
the other from Ontario in Canada. Outside the capital city of
Peru there is a community of squatters one hundred thousand in number, some from the slums of the city, some from
the villages of the interior where they had no future. They
settled on public land and built for themselves huts with
straw mats for walls and roofs. They have one cold-water tap
for thirty families. The sewer is a ditch at the side of the road.
Schools available can take only a portion of the children. The
men do odd jobs in the city and earn perhaps a hundred
dollars in a year. Set alongside that the capital city of Ontario,
Canada, where there was a two-month strike by high school
teachers at the end of 1975. They had been offered an increase in pay of 39 percent over two years. They were strik-

ing for 45 percent. That would assure them of better than $25,000 a year after eight years' experience. It was of no significance to them that their government was pleading for restraint in order to reduce the rate of inflation that was steadily impoverishing so many in the population. Ironically, a decision of the national board controlling prices and wages eventually reduced their increase below what had been originally offered.

How long can we enjoy our affluence and continually cry for more while elsewhere in our world whole populations sink ever deeper into poverty and misery? We use our intelligence and a billion of our dollars to have a look at the rocks and dust on Mars. That is an exciting scientific project. The problem of what is to be done about the deepening poverty of large sections of our world is much less intriguing. The situation calls for citizens whose faith forces them to look beyond their own borders and to begin thinking about what economic justice requires, not just in their own land but in their world.

Perhaps no better example of our political blindness could be found than the way in which our Western nations have dealt with the problems of the Middle East. A succession of wars has already cost Israel, Syria, and Egypt billions of dollars that were desperately needed for the welfare of their people and has devastated the cities of Lebanon. And there is as little prospect of peace as in Northern Ireland.

But do we remember how all this came to happen? In 1914–1918 we were fighting a war in Europe and the Middle East and the Allies needed both Jewish and Arab support. So two promises were made concerning Palestine, then a part of the Ottoman Empire, inhabited largely by Arabs but in a sadly neglected condition. There was a promise to Arabs that, if they aided us in the war, they would have control in Palestine, and there was a promise to the Jews, the Balfour Declaration, guaranteeing British support for the establishment of a Jewish national home in Palestine. Perhaps to the negotiators the two promises were not considered to be necessarily in conflict. Perhaps they assumed that the Arabs generously would put no obstacles in the way of the Jewish homeland. But they were cautious not to let either of the parties know what had been promised to the other. Jewish representation in Britain was both strong and influential. Arab representatives when they went to London could barely secure a hearing.

At first the Arabs welcomed Jewish settlers, but with the Jewish purchase of large blocks of land and, with the rise of Jewish terrorist organizations proclaiming on their banners their intention of taking over Palestine, Arab fears and opposition became intense. Then, in the '30s, when the pressures on Jews in Russia, Eastern Europe, and Germany became severe and they had to find homes elsewhere if they were to live, they were encouraged by our governments to go to Palestine rather than to make their homes in countries such as ours. Boatloads of Jews fleeing in terror from Europe sought entry at port after port in the Western world and were turned away. Thousands eventually found illegal entry into Palestine, thereby heightening the tensions between Jew and Arab.

For thirty years we let that problem simmer, accepting no real responsibility for what was happening, a problem that was of our own contriving. Then, when in 1948 it began to explode with disastrous results, we professed to be surprised and shocked at the conduct of both Jew and Arab. We Christians let it happen, in our blindness but also with one eye open to our own interest, and now we sit in judgment on both Israeli and Arab for their unwillingness to be at peace with each other! It is hard to escape the impression that we did not take the trouble to look very carefully at what we were doing with the destinies of some millions of Jews and Arabs, who of course were none of them Christians. Would we have dealt as carelessly with them had they been Christians? Would someone then have spoken out on their behalf?

That carelessness and callousness about the fate of non-Christians becomes even more disturbing when we consider the Holocaust, in which six million Jewish men, women, and children perished—in the land where Protestantism had its birth and where our Western civilization produced some of its richest developments. Emil Fackenheim is right when he says that we Christians are much too eager to forget it. The latest ploy in that direction is to call attention to the fact that twenty million Russians perished in the war and to ask, "What is a mere six million in comparison with that?" But there is a difference between dying in defense of one's country and being the victims of a cold-blooded attempt to expunge Israel from membership in the human family.

To our embarrassment, more recent investigations have revealed that many thousands of Jews could have been saved had our governments been willing to cooperate. One illustration has been given by Dr. Fackenheim. Before the invasion of Holland there were Jewish Hollanders in the Dutch Air Force being trained in Canada who asked the Canadian government to permit their families to come to Canada in order to be safe should Hitler enter Holland. The permission was refused on the grounds that after the war they might not be willing to leave. It is incredible. And all of them perished. We can say, "We did not know," but why did we not know? Looking back, what one remembers is a deadly silence about the whole matter until it was part of the past about which one could do nothing. But why was there that silence? One cannot believe that it was either necessary or accidental. And the Christian church as watchman had a responsibility to know and to sound the warning. The Holocaust took place in a civilization that, though it had long been proud to call itself Christian, for centuries had been tolerant of an anti-Semitism that every so often blazed out in a murderous fashion. Our civilization right here in North America is still far too tolerant of that same sixteen-hundred-year-old social poison. Scratch the surface of ten Christians and you are likely to find it slumbering in at least eight of them. How recently have you heard a sermon, or, if you are a minister, have you preached a sermon, that would be likely to conquer that anti-Semitism in at least a few persons, or that would effectively open the possibility of understanding and solidarity between Jew and Christian, a solidarity that should exist between two peoples who have so many common roots?

Racial discrimination belongs also in the indictment. Who that rejoices in the advances of the last twenty years does not feel shame at the blindness that for centuries prevented Christians from seeing what they were doing to other human beings close at hand? Discrimination was woven so deeply into the whole culture that it had become part of the world that one took for granted. But that is the kind of evil that the Christian revelation is specially designed to unmask. Yet even when the unmasking had begun and the Christian conscience was at least disturbed, the attitude in general tended to be: "Don't hurry us. This is a deep-seated problem and we are going to solve it eventually if you just give us time." But one day the black man said: "There is no more time. We have been patient for three hundred years and now we want what it is our right to have." Even then very little happened until one day the cities began to burn and white citizens, Christians and others, suddenly realized that on this issue it was judgment day. There really *was* no more time. But why should it have been so hard for white Christians to accept a black man or woman as a fellow citizen and a fellow human being? Blindness, blindness, blindness, and, as some black theologians are laying bare, a blindness that has theological as well as racial and economic roots and requires of us some theological repentance and reorientation if it is to be decisively overcome.

And then there was Vietnam. Our concern here is not with the wickedness of that war but with the blindness of Christians to what was happening in their world. Most of us became conscious that there was a serious problem in Vietnam about the year 1963! Even then we did not take it very seriously. It was not clear how we came to be so intimately involved in a civil war in a distant Southeast Asian country and few of us took the trouble to find out. The popular impression was that the Free World was being threatened there by Communist China and we must spring to freedom's defense or country after country in Southeast Asia would topple into the Communist block. But in 1963 the struggle in Vietnam had already been in progress eighteen years! Why did we not know? Why were Christians so poorly informed about what storms were brewing in their world? The war in Vietnam will go down in history as the war that did not need to be—and the primary responsibility for its occurrence will rest, surprisingly, not upon the United States but upon Britain and France. During the war of 1939–1945, French Indochina became the possession of our enemies, the Vichy French and the Japanese. Ho Chi Minh and his Viet Minh freedom fighters were an underground guerrilla force in alliance with us and hoping that the reward of victory for them would be an independent Vietnam, free of French colonial rule. In 1945, Ho Chi Minh with the assistance of Chiang Kai-shek's army was able to free the north and establish there a republic that at first was recognized by the French. He also gained control of the three key cities of the south, which meant that he was on the verge of unifying the whole country. But De Gaulle, eager to restore France's power, would not permit this. The French laid claim anew to the territory and an English general, Sir Douglas Gracey, in cooperation with the French, and with the help of Japanese prisoners who were released from prison camps, drove the northern forces out of the south, giving it back into control of France.

The period after 1945 was a time when Western nations were surrendering their colonial possessions in the East to native rule. India received its independence from Britain and Indonesia from Holland. But France was determined to retain Vietnam. Now began a nine years' war to reconquer the north, to destroy the new republic and unite the land once more under French colonial rule.

The emergence of Communist China in 1949 and the Korean war in 1950 earned France's policy in Vietnam the sympathy and support of Britain and the United States. But the venture proved to be one of the most wasteful and disastrous wars in France's history. By 1950, France was in danger of bankrupting itself and was ready to give up the fight to recover the north, but Britain and the United States, fearful of one more Communist land in Asia, urged her to continue, and the United States began to make large financial contributions to the French expenses of the war. By 1954 the United States was paying almost the total cost of the French effort. But, defeated at Dien-Bien-Phu, the French gave up, retired to the south, and, with the United States continuing to pay the cost of government in the south, began to surrender control of the area and to let it become an American dependency.

It was still nine years short of 1963. We do not need to trace the rest of the sad history, sad for both Vietnam and the United States. What is relevant here is that for eighteen years we Christians were ignorant of a disaster that was in process and for which year by year as citizens we were going to be increasingly responsible. Why did we not know? How could the policies and actions of Britain, France, and the United States be actions in the dark so far as we were concerned? We were morally blind for eighteen years, and some Christians are still blind to what they let happen for those nearly thirty years. Again one must ask, Would we have remained blind so long if those thirty-nine million Vietnamese had been white? Christian? Protestant? Anglo-Saxon? White Protestants in Asia struggling for political independence in 1945 might have been quite appealing!

There is no need to stretch the indictment farther. It could go much farther. We might note the silence of Christians in cities such as Montreal and Boston, which for years have let their raw sewage pour ceaselessly into the public waters. Or we might ask why American Christians have protested so feebly the escalation of defense costs from thirteen and a half billions in 1950 to more than one hundred billions in 1976, during twenty-six years of what the modern world calls relative peace. When one reads in Khrushchev's memoirs of his sorrow at the Russian population's deprivation in regard to food and housing, one wonders whether in our blindness we have not missed opportunities for escape from this Frankenstein monster that gobbles up the resources of friend and foe alike.

WHY THIS BLINDNESS?

We must inquire now why we Christians have been so dilatory in the exercise of our watchman function in the twentieth-century world. Why in our blindness have we stumbled into so many disasters for ourselves and others? We must ask because it is so clearly a tradition from which we must be liberated if we are to face the future with confidence.

First is the narrowing of the Christian's vision by pietism, which makes him concentrate his concern upon the soul, the inner life, and pay too little heed to what is happening in the outer life, the public and the international life. Or the separation between church and state may be such that, while the gospel is heeded with the deepest earnestness in church and private life, some form of civil religion is applied with equal earnestness in public life. False distinctions between what is sacred and what is secular go into operation here. Only what is sacred is appropriate in the church. And what is happening politically or economically in some other part of the world seems obviously too secular to be discussed in the precincts of the church. A line is drawn between the church and the world that permits Christians with a good conscience to remain ignorant of what is happening in their world. Their care for the souls of men and women frees them of responsibility for what is happening to those same men and women in the public realm. But there is no escape from responsibility for what is happening. Decisions are constantly being made in our communities, and even the total silence of Christians is a form of political decision. It is a decision not to interfere with the policy that is dominant.

We have emphasized throughout the part played by the long-standing illusion that we are citizens of Christian countries and that our Western civilization is Christian civilization. The idea of Christendom, of a society and culture so leavened by the Christian gospel that it is essentially Christian in distinction from a pagan world beyond it, dies hard. It was, and still is, productive of an optimism that has identified the signs of progress in our society with the dawning of God's kingdom on earth. The church has been under pressure to sustain that optimism, to "think positively" and to refrain from any word or action that would create doubts about the benevolent character of our progress.

In the '20s of this century the kingdom seemed to be just beyond the next hill. We were almost there. One more big push—in missions, in social reform, in the spread of pacifism, in church unification—and the kingdom would be here. And even when what was just beyond the next hill proved to be the cruelty and inhumanity of diverse kinds of tyranny, the optimism still persisted in the churches. The intellectual mood outside the churches becoming with the years increasingly grim and despairing, the contrast between the two moods was not at all to the advantage of the churches. It may have been responsible for the air of unreality that plagued the language heard within the churches as the century advanced, which in turn contributed to the alienation of many from the church's worship and fellowship. And from outside and inside alike came the demand that the church should maintain an unfaltering cheerfulness about the future.

THE DECEPTIVENESS OF IDEALISM

In this optimistic religion, so supportive of progress and prosperity, there was frequently more idealism than gospel. In fact, a form of moral idealism tended to displace the Christian gospel. It was easier, and more certain of success, to

preach about ideals than about repentance and reconcilia-
tion. But ideals, stripped of their glamour, have actually the
same content as laws, and moral idealism is theologically a
legalism only slightly concealed. The law says, "You shall not
steal," where the idealist says that he cherishes the ideal of
honesty. The law is rude, confronting us with the humbling
demand to confess whether we have been dishonest. But
idealism is more lenient, allowing us to congratulate ourselves that we cherish the ideal of honesty, no matter what
the character of our conduct may have been.

It is not accidental that the word "ideal" does not occur in
Scripture. It belongs in a very different tradition and a very
different theological context, one that takes a much more
optimistic and less realistic view of human nature. The idealist expects to be judged not by his conduct but by the character of his ideals. A Biblical faith encourages no such illusions
about the self. A person *is* what he *does*. The laws of God
measure not our self-estimate but something much more
concrete and real, our conduct. A Biblical faith calls us to
judge ourselves by the same law that we use in judging others. Idealism, however, encourages a double standard. The
idealist expects his own worth to be evaluated by the quality
of his ideals but, when he himself judges others, he measures
them and their conduct by the extent to which they come up
to or fall below the standard of his ideals.

Two instances will show how easily this type of idealism
can lead to deceptive judgments. Both stem from the period
directly after World War II. The newspaper one night carried a report of a Russian warship putting in at an Italian port.
The sailors went ashore and mingled with the citizens. This
was at once interpreted as an aggressive Russian action attempting to create sympathy with Communism in a democratic country. Soon afterward came a report of an American
warship visiting an Italian port and the sailors mingling with
the citizens, but this was declared to be a praiseworthy contribution to international friendship. What made the difference? Our ideals justified our action! Where the Russian aim

was to mislead, ours was to create brotherhood! But to the neutral onlooker the two actions were identical and with an identical motivation. The second incident also concerned similar actions by Russian and American representatives. One evening in 1945 there appeared in a Philadelphia newspaper the pictures of two German atomic scientists. The report said that these two scientists had been "lured" by generous Russian promises to make their homes in Russia and to work on the Russian atomic projects. This was conduct unworthy of an ally and to be roundly condemned. Two weeks later there appeared in the same paper the pictures of three German atomic scientists who had expressed their delight at being invited with their families to America to work on the American atomic projects. This was a stroke of good fortune both for them and for us that would move our project much more swiftly forward. The action was praised in the highest terms.

These two parallel reports were laid before a group of Christian workers, men of no mean caliber, and with only one exception the response was: "But surely you do not judge our action on the same basis as the Russian action. The similarity is only on the surface. Everyone knows that their intention is to use atomic power for the subjugation of the human race to a Communist order, and everyone knows equally that the ideals to which we are committed guarantee that we shall use atomic energy only for the benefit of the human race." George Kennan, no advocate of softness toward Communism, blasts this double standard in an interview with Martin Agronsky in *The New York Review of Books,* Jan. 20, 1977. Pointing out that the United States sold Iran, on the border of Russia, nine billion dollars of arms in 1976 and with the arms sent along thousands of technicians, he asks the question how the American government and citizens would view similar shipments by Russia to Mexico.

It is very difficult for an individual idealist, or an idealistic church, or an idealistic nation, to achieve self-knowledge. The idealist finds it almost impossible to take his place on the penitent bench alongside all the other sinners in the world. His ideals exempt him from the judgment of God—and justify him, so that he is in no need of an utterly humbling justification by faith. It is significant that civil religion is almost totally idealistic in character. But so also is much of the religion prevalent in the church and the synagogue!

Yet another factor in the blindness of Christians and in their failure to resist disastrous evils has been a certain passivity in regard to the larger events of history, a kind of fatalism that arises actually from a misunderstanding of the sovereignty of God. God's sovereignty means for them God's control of all that happens. They are aware that human beings make things happen. They themselves are responsible for most of what happens in their lives. But in the larger sphere of world events, the movements that produce the main events of history, developments that the individual seems helpless to oppose, and disasters that are inescapable, they recognize events as acts of God. The alternatives for them seem to be either a God who is in direct control of history or no God at all.

It does not occur to them that God's sovereignty in human affairs must be understood in the light of the cross of Christ. The cross is the product of human blindness and evil. Men erect the cross—self-righteous men angered by what met them in Jesus, fearful men anxious for the future of their religious and political establishment, blind men not able to see what they are doing. But when men have done all that they can do, another Will becomes manifest, determining the actual and ultimate meaning of the event in history. God is in the event in the sense that in binding this Jesus so completely to himself and making him the revelation of his inmost nature as a God of righteousness and love, he made inevitable the clash with human wills that resulted in the cross. And God is sovereign in the event, not in making it happen but in determining its meaning for the world, transforming it from a sheer disaster into the climactic and central event of the whole history of redemption.

At the cross all passivity and fatalism in relation to the events of history are purged from the Christian. His eyes are opened to the dread possibility that, like a Caiaphas or a Pilate or a Judas, he should let his political, economic, or religious loyalties make him strike out blindly against God. What has happened in history is what we human beings have willed should happen. We have to take the full responsibility for it. And there is no possibility of a different kind of history —a new age of justice and mercy—until the will within us is confronted and conquered by the will of God that meets us so compellingly in the Christ of the cross.

The tragedy of the church in the twentieth century has been this persistent blindness, a blindness that has kept it from performing its watchman function over an endangered world. The blind have been leading the blind and both have fallen into the ditch, a very deep and ruinous ditch. But how is such blindness to be overcome? The answer is revelation, a revelation that has in it the hope of redemption. Revelation is not an abstruse or abstract theological doctrine. It is the opening of the eyes of human beings to see the truth about themselves, their neighbors, their community, their world in the light of what God is doing in the midst of time. But for that opening of our eyes we are dependent upon the great succession of persons whose eyes God opened to himself and to the realities of life and whose witness is preserved for us in the Scriptures. It was John Calvin who coined the pertinent saying that the Scriptures are the spectacles that all of us need to correct the astigmatism that distorts our vision.

Nothing could be more contradictory than the authority and centrality that are attributed officially to the Scriptures in the church and the triviality and ineffectiveness of their use. This is as true in conservative churches as in liberal ones. The Bible alone of all books is before the congregation in worship. Most sermons at least make a bow toward it. The ritual is usually full of it. Church school lessons get their major content from it. Millions of copies of it in various translations are sold each year. Thousands of Christian and Jewish scholars work constantly at its interpretation. Yet anyone familiar with the members of a local congregation knows how elementary and superficial is the understanding of Scripture among most of them. Only a tiny percentage have any interest in exploring the Scriptures with the help of twentieth-century scholarship. Still tinier is the number who in an educational program can open up to others the significance of the Scriptures for present-day issues. The most that seems to be expected of Christians is that they may read a few verses of Scripture daily in private devotions for their inner enrichment.

Even among ministers there is little awareness that almost every part of Scripture is addressed to *communities* and is not rightly heard until it is heard by the Christian community. Again, the popularity of topical sermons and the comparative ease with which they can be prepared discourages ministers from undertaking the more difficult task of letting the ancient texts come alive in the modern situation. Few seem to be aware how ironical it is and how perilous for the church that in the twentieth-century Biblical scholarship should have made such huge strides forward and at the same time the Bible should have been receiving less and less attention in the program of the church and in the lives of Christian people. A church that has lost its access to the Scriptures is a church with seriously defective vision. (See my book, *The Strange Silence of the Bible in the Church,* for a detailed investigation of this problem.)

The word "hermeneutics," which has had a currency of late for the area of interpretation, has at least the virtue of suggesting that the understanding of Scripture is a more complicated undertaking than most Christians recognize. The road from ancient text to present meaning has on it many pitfalls that can obstruct, distort, and falsify the words of the original witnesses. There is no simple, easy route either back into the ancient situations where the words were first spoken or written, or forward from there into our own situations in the world of today, where they must be so translated that they have their original enlightening and transforming power. A remark of the Marburg scholar, Ernst Fuchs, is pertinent here. In one of those books of his that are so hard to read, he makes at one point the simple but explosive remark: we have not yet captured the meaning of Biblical words in our present-day sermons and lectures unless it is as dangerous in our situation to speak them as it was for the original Biblical spokesmen!

The outcome of such openness to and immersion in the Scriptures for the Christian is that prophets, psalmists, wise men, apostles, evangelists, and above all Jesus Christ become his most intimate companions, tutors, and guides, and their watchman function becomes his. But to be a watchman on behalf of his community, his nation, his world is to be a critical theologian and to see below the surface issues of our time the faith issues where the ultimate decisions are really made. To be a responsible Christian citizen one must in some measure be a responsible theologian. It is high time that theology should cease to be locked up in theological schools as a concern only of specialists, and should become a normal activity and interest of the local congregation. Theology that knows its own task is not concerned with abstruse questions far above the level and the interests of ordinary church members and of the man in the street. It belongs at the heart of the church, where as churchmen we face honestly the contradiction between what we profess to be and what we are. We profess to be the body of Jesus Christ, a community of persons so bonded to each other and to him by our faith that he is able in us to be the judging, reconciling, and redeeming Word of God that is needed to rescue our world from the confusion and peril it has created for itself.

But we are something much less than that, and the task of a theology "in the church, for the church and by the church" should be to help us see more clearly where the line runs between faithfulness and unfaithfulness, between justice and injustice, between an uncompromising faith and a religion deeply compromised by its cultural involvements. Life in the twentieth century under the sign of the cross is not what comes naturally for us. We are much more comfortable with a civil religion that provides us with principles and ideals that point the way to success in both personal and national life. But comfort, success, or even national unity is hardly a first concern of any thoughtful Christian.